DIVINE TRAGEDY

DIVINE TRAGEDY

MEHMET TANBERK

DIVINE TRAGEDY

iUniverse books may be ordered through
booksellers or by contacting:

iUniverse
1663 Liberty Drive
Bloomington, IN 47403
www.iuniverse.com
1-800-Authors (1-800-288-4677)

ISBN: 978-1-4917-8311-5 (sc)
ISBN: 978-1-4917-8312-2 (e)

Print information available on the last page.

iUniverse rev. date: 12/28/2015

CONTENTS

FOREWORD

In the fall of 2008, the people of Istanbul had formed long queues in front of the Sakip Sabanci museum. The schools were encouraging their students, to see the works of one of the art geniuses of the 20th century, by hiring busses. Museum administration, after exhibiting Picasso a year ago, had succeeded to bring one of the Salvadore Dali collections to Istanbul. The citizens of Istanbul, fond of art, had shown an overwhelming interest to the exhibition.

I had to wait for half an hour, in front of the gate to get access to the museum halls. From the very moment of looking at the initial art pieces, one could realize the geniality of Dali. He had not only drawn the physical world but the realm of imagination as well. He had not only used paints but all kind of materials. Dali had worked like a psychiatrist when drew how people had wild dreams when they were in love. He had benefited from the definitions of Dante, when decided to depict heaven and hell. This coincidence provoked me to read the Italian classics like Dante's Divine Comedy and Boccaccio's Decameron. I read both of them in a short time with partial disappointment. Could we have access to after world life, when walking in a forest, as Dante defined? Could the story of mankind be limited only to the betraying males and females, as Boccaccio has told? Some sort of Decameron stories should have been retold reflecting the recent human kind experiences. History behind the closed doors could be left to the imagination of fiction teller, making all characters part of the history. Why there should not be a logical pathway between actual and after world life beyond all religious explanations? In such an attempt the name of my new book would be surely different from Dante's Divine Comedy, as:

DIVINE TRAGEDY

1

SULTAN HAMID EXECUTES HIS VIZIER

Ottoman Empire was founded at the beginning of the 14th century and continuously expanded till the 17th century in Asia, Africa and Europe. That long of a life span was not a common case in history. Starting from the 18th century, the empire started to decline. Sultans felt obliged to start reformation to stop or at least slow down the decline. The first time in 1839, sultan Abdülmecit declared restoration of the justice system, recognizing the civil rights of citizens. Janissaries, the official army of the empire, were not used to obeying the rules. Their habit was to dethrone the sultans, whenever something displeased them, whatever it might cost the state. The Empire was losing territories in three continents. The old army was replaced with a disciplined one. Sultan Abdülhamid II, opened the new parliament in 1876 to calm down the public resistance. He could not, however stick to the democratic rules too long. He abolished the parliament in 1877. The people were now being caught and executed by secret journal reports without interrogation.

In those days a rumor spread in the palace about the execution of a well esteemed vizier (pasha). The palace folk were chatting about this execution in a banquet.

- Dear vizier brothers. Our deceased pasha had gone too far. He was disobeying the sultan by initiating uncommon reformations wherever he has been assigned.
- Of course I knew him. He was someone obstinate to act the way he liked.
- If you are too rigid in state affairs, you should always expect some disasters.
  Banquet had finished and attendants started to leave. Only one of them was stopped by the sultan.
- Don't go Hamid aga. I want to talk to you. You saw how insincere my subjects were, didn't you?
- What can they do, your majesty? They are afraid of you. Because of the denunciation system you have set forth. As you can see, it works against you now. All your loyal men are being pretentious towards you, for their well-being. You can never learn the truth, nor can you rely on anybody.
- You may be right. But if they cannot tell the truth, can they not stay silent as you did? You did not like the execution either, did you?

- I knew the deceased pasha as a patriotic, honest man.
- He was, Hamid. But unfortunately all patriotic and honest men, have not always been good for the country. Unrealistic ambitions, untimely initiatives and lack of experiences sometimes may drive the country to disaster while the inherent intention is decent, to save it. If you sit in a coffee house and listen to the people, everybody suggests something new to save the country. They are unrealistic, but harmless people to their own country. But the real harmful ones are those who hold a position in state. They are ambitious for their personal progress by trying adventurous attempts.
- Your majesty, you do not mean our deceased pasha, was one of them. Do you? I knew him as a devoted man.
- I fully agree with you Hamid. All his plans were realistic and necessary things. But do you know, what his mistake was? He misjudged the order of his actions. Of course upgrading the quality of our schools is one of our first priorities. Of course we cannot continue the sultanate without changing the Empire to a republic, sooner or later. But if you search for democracy first and education afterwards, you will fail like France did. They dethroned the king, for the sake of liberty, equality and fraternity. They unfortunately

had to accept an Empire which was ruled without liberty and equality, after these good wishes.

- But your majesty, you also came to throne with the claim of liberty and equality. You even first founded the parliament but abolished it a year later. Will our country not be a democracy like England?

- Look Hamid, Oxford and Cambridge universities. They are active since 700 years, renewing their education systems always in line with the scientific progress. We are still teaching in our religious schools, with 1400 years old knowledge. England freed herself from religious conservatism 500 years ago. We are still far away keeping up with contemporary values. My father started and I tried to continue to modernize our schools. In his time, Robert College and other English teaching schools were opened. I added French, German and Italian high schools and colleges. Academies to teach engineering, political sciences, pharmacology, medicine and fine arts were all put into function during my sultanate. Osman Hamdi bey founded archaeology museum also in my time. You see Hamid. I tried to pave of the path of high education to lead us to democracy in the future. If we do not wait for the well installment of these institutions our democracy will be interrupted, first by the military and then by the politicians.

- Do we have that long time your majesty?

- We need as long time as our people are sufficiently educated to change and adapt themselves, without destructive resistance. British universities educated English people to act unemotionally and rationally. When Cromwell changed the monarchy to democracy by Magna Carta he did not destroy the country's elite. The king stayed to represent the state without much authority. House of Lords continued the nobility of the British Empire. I am afraid our people are of the opinion to follow the French style. They think they can progress by demolishing everything, like what has been done in the French revolution. They do not even know what to replace when the old is discontinued. We are no longer proud of being an Ottoman. Younger generations put more emphasis on ethnicity rather than the humanity. That's why our Empire will soon disintegrate.

- Once we were proud of being an Ottoman. Where did we make mistake your majesty to get weaker and poorer?

- We have not made one, but two mistakes Hamid. The first and the foremost mistake was to bring the printing machine three centuries later. Due to the delay, Ottomans remained illiterate, and fell behind in science and innovation. We had a strong navy and talented captains like Piri Reis who drew the first map of the world and Hayreddin pasha who defeated papal navy under the commandment of Andrea Doria, all through the 16th century. We neglected to sail out to the hot seas and this way deprived the empire of colonialistic expansions.

- Your majesty I am speechless against your wisdom and experience. I still do not like it when some people call you a murderer. We shared many happy days in our childhood. My name was given by your father after you. I remember now, we could not watch the sacrificed animals on religious days and used to run away from the palace. How can such a kind man like you be called murderer?

- You are right Hamid. We both could not watch bloodshed. But you were lucky to become a servant in the palace. I was unlucky to become the sultan of the land. I can predict with anxiety, what those people, who call me murderer now, will do in a close future. They will drive the young generation, on whom I spend so much effort for their education, to unnecessary wars just for their own fame and ambitions. At the end of the day, young men will go to graves instead of attending universities. The development and enrichment of the country will be delayed for further times ahead. I am asking you Hamid. Those who order thousands to die, will not be murderers and sultans executing one or two harmful pashas like me, will be called criminal, is that fair?

2

THE PALACE LIFE OF HAMID AGA

The father of Hamid aga was the chief cook of sultan Abdulmecid. He was closer to the sultan more than many of the viziers. He was the main taster of food to protect sultan against the poisoning. He was also responsible to prepare the menu in banquets to domestic and foreign visitors. He used to train all kitchen personnel to cook the dishes and mind their manners in services. He had the last say about the price and quality of the goods purchased to the kitchens.

Sultan Abdulmecid had liked Dervish aga so much that when both had a son in the same year 1842, he named both boys, as Hamid. They were raised together in the palace gardens. Prince Hamid had liked his namesake, the son of the chief cook and made him his best friend. At the age of four, their interest was the horses in the palace stable and decorated royal coaches. Chief groom Veysel aga used to make them ride on young ponies together with his daughter Pakize.

She was one year younger but still good friend of the boys. It was great fun for the prince and Hamid to hide themselves from Pakize to make her look for them and cry when she fails. At the end of the game the prince used to reward both Hamid and Pakize either with candy or a doll.

Hamid attended the same palace school as the primary one. In 1860 he graduated from the college and started to work in the kitchen with his father who was proud of his son. Unfortunately he passed away at the end of the year. Sultan assigned young Hamid as the chief cook to replace his father. He was young, handsome and a successful servant in the palace. His mother Mesude hatun did not have any difficulty to find a match for her son. He married with his childhood friend Pakize, who had been the preferred servant of one of the princesses in harem.

The marriage brought great happiness to young Hamid. In the meantime the old sultan had died. His successor Abdülaziz left him in the same position. In 1862 his son Ali was born. With the permission of sultan he attended the palace school.

When Ali graduated primary school, Sultan called them.

- Hamid aga what do you think about your son now?
- I want to enroll him to my school, your majesty.
- No Hamid aga. If we let, the bright young men like Ali, continue in the same school we graduated, how can we expect progress in Empire? You will send him to Robert College which has opened recently, so that he will learn English as a foreign language.

By the order of sultan, Ali began studying at Robert College in 1873. He would never forget his first day at school. His father Hamid aga had taken him to the school. When they climbed the hill from Bebek coast they thought they were in the palace garden. Ali would be a boarding student. Hamid aga wished to see where his son would stay. They visited classes, dormitories, the dining hall and the sporting facilities. Right at that time Hamid aga understood, why the west was ahead of the oriental countries. He was obliged to the sultan for his guidance. In 1876, his namesake and childhood friend, Abdulhamid had been the sultan.

3

UNION & PROGRESS PARTY

Towards the end of the 19th century some young military officers in Salonica, gathered secretly in a house at a remote district of the city. They discussed the situation of the empire. They all had imaginations broader than fairy tales and ambitions deeper than the oceans.

- How do you see the situation in the Balkans?
- Disaster, not just in the Balkans, the Sultan is almost enslaved to the British. They exploit the Suez Canal as they wish and our sultan remains silent. Most of the barefoot Arabs are against sultan who takes no initiative to teach them their status. How long can patriotic Turks stand against this humiliation?
- What really annoys me is, none of us, the patriotic Turks do enjoy the freedom as our one time subjects do now. To express the thoughts is forbidden, to criticize is dangerous.
- O.K. guys. Shall we just simply watch?

- Of course not. Untimely moves may be risky but waiting too long might be too late. We should wait for the proper moment. Let us organize secretly for some time and collect members for our organization among the young people.
- I think that is a very good idea. We can this way have time to fix our strategies to overthrow sultan Hamid to make the country a land of free people.
- Say we did it. Who is going to replace him?
- Why not to be princes Mehmet Reshad or Vahidettin?
- They say Mehmet Reshad has no experience.
- This is not important because we shall help him. If he hands over all his authority to us, things will go better.
- I fully share this idea. Ottoman Empire should be ruled by the younger generations.
- O.K. friends. Should we not select one of us, as the leader of this movement?
- We all have the necessary qualities to run the leadership, have we not friends? Let us think about this issue after overthrowing the sultan. When all countrymen are freed the rest will be easy.
- Are you not missing one point friends? You want to overthrow a sultan and replace him with another one. What will change then?
- If we bring someone to the head of State from the Ottoman dynasty he can hold the whole Muslim

world together under the caliph. We shall then be more influential Mustafa.

- Do you mean if the Empire has a dispute with Britain, France or Russia, our religious brethren will run to help?
- Have we not supported them over the centuries?
- I will not be able to share this optimism. Look at yourself. You are the young military officers supported by sultan over the years. You are still planning to overthrow him in the first opportune time. Why should, non-Turkish subjects not do the same, following a stronger nation rather than the weaker Ottoman Empire?
- Will such a betrayal not be against their best interests?
- Why should it be? What happened to Mehmet pasha of Kavala? His dynasty still rules the Egypt. When the people see stronger and wealthier, they change.
- When we make an alliance with the Germans, we shall be stronger. Non-Turkish people will know who to support.
- My dear dreamers. By forming an alliance with the Germans you can win against France but never Britain. They are dominant over the seas. None of the territorial empires can reach the borders of British Empire nor beat the world wide logistic advantages of England.
- Do you suggest that we do not take any part?

- Why should we not be completely neutral? By your choice if Germans win in an international dispute, Ottoman Empire will be a German colony. But if Germans lose, there will be no Ottoman Empire.

4

THE YOUNGHOOD OF ALI EFENDI

Ali's school life was progressing better than expectations. He was always getting best grades in his classes. He had friends from the richest families in his classes and dormitory. He had won school championships in sporting activities. Sultan invited him to the palace when there were foreign visitors, and a reliable translator was required. He used to spend week-ends at the palace near his family. Veysel aga was proud of his grandson. He was always providing him well breed horses from the palace stable. Years passed quickly and the graduation year came along. Sultan Abdulhamid was interested in his higher education as a promising young man to contribute to the country. When the Sultan met the German ambassador he recalled Ali. In those years Germany was one of the most advanced countries in Engineering. He requested the Ambassador to arrange for Ali to attend a university in Germany.

Hamid aga was surprised when sultan called Ali and him together. Sultan explained.

- Ali, next year, in 1885 you will be the graduate of Robert College. I am pleased with your achievements because you are the generation I wished to see for the future of the Empire. Do you have any plans for your future?
- No majesty, I don't.
- But I do have Ali. I am planning to establish a university to teach all sorts of engineering sciences. I will need well trained teachers to teach in this school. I selected you as one of them. But I want you to learn this science in the best place, I mean Germany. If you go there you will not only get the best education. But you will also learn German as second language. Do you accept my proposal?
- You gave me the greatest honor and opportunity your majesty. I shall soon start to investigate the enrollment conditions.
- No Ali, you will not need to do anything. I already enrolled you to Berlin Technical University. You will start next year.

When Hamid aga and Ali went home, they gave the good news to Pakize hatun. She was both proudly happy and motherly worried. What would such a handsome young man do in Germany alone? She started to look for a proper match for her son and she found one in a short time. Fatma, the daughter of Nusret pasha, was famous in the Harem for her beauty. After graduating from primary school she had been the servant of the lady members of the palace. In a short time, the families agreed. Sultan ordered a palace wedding, for the young couple with the invitation of all high level bureaucrats and palace servants.

In the fall of 1885 Ali and Fatma moved to their house, a rented flat in Berlin. They were happy during the first month, when Ali had not yet started studying. They visited many places in Berlin at weekends when Ali did not have German lessons. After sufficiently visiting Berlin's sights, they travelled to different German cities over the week ends like Hamburg, Nurnberg, Frankfurt and Heidelberg. They were admiring the beauty and discipline of Germany and German people every day.

At last Ali started university. Difficult days began for Fatma. She had nobody to chat with. She had refused to take German lessons although Ali had insisted very much. All teachers were male and she had been traditionally raised, not to spend long hours with men even for the sake of education. It was also difficult to accept for Fatma that Ali had a lot of girl friends from school, visiting them to study the home work and join the week end programs. Fatma soon regretted of not having taken German lessons. There were nobody among Ali's friends who could talk Turkish. She had to watch them when they laugh or become serious in some cases.

She was like palace servants not to talk but only wait to serve. At last she did what she knew best. She became pregnant. Now she had been the center of interest. Everybody was curious about her health and was asking questions about her pregnancy which was noticed with her belly. In the fall of 1886 their son Hasan was born.

All of the obsessions and complexes of Fatma had disappeared. She no longer minded Ali's girl friends nor did she care about being unnoticed because she was not able to talk and understand the people around her. To change the underwear of her son, to feed him, to make him sleep and to wash him were all fun she needed. Ali was also often at home rather than being with his friends. When Hasan started to crawl, their baby sitting duties multiplied. Ali was now responsible for shopping for house hold items as well as the needs of the baby. When Hasan started to walk they hired Helga to assist Fatma for daily work. She was a reliable and clever 18 year old girl, who had lost her family and was all alone in life. She was very provocative to communicate with Fatma. She had no problem to understand Fatma. She knew from her stares and gesticulation what Fatma meant. In 6 months' time Fatma could understand, even answer a little bit in German. She had overcome a bit of her language problems by the help of Helga.

Now, mostly Helga was taking care of Hasan, even taking him to the park in his pram. Fatma was very pleased with her service because her son started to learn German from Helga as his native language. Hasan was talented like most little babies. He could speak Turkish with his parents and unmistakably speak German with Helga. He realized after a while that his father knew German and never spoke Turkish with his father. In 1889 Ali registered his son to a kindergarten close to their house. Hasan was very pleased with the new set up. He had many friends in the pre-school with whom he could play all day long. Fatma now had plenty of leisure time. She used to walk on the streets of this beautiful city in good weather and go shopping when the weather was bad.

On a hot spring day Fatma was alone in the park, and saw a woman who called out to her son in Turkish.

- Excuse me, are you a Turk?
- Yes I am and here with my husband since two years.
- My husband attends engineering school. We have been here close to four years. I have one son who goes to pre-school.

- How do you spend your time here?
- Oh, don't remind me. I have been here in Berlin since two years and still can't learn to speak German. My husband is a military attaché in the Embassy. Many of his friends are Germans or bachelors. I am getting bored of having no one to talk to.
- You are lucky. My husband has only German friends in the school. I could practice some German from Helga, the daily servant of our family. It was good to meet you. At least we can get together on some days.
- I would love to. My name is Fevziye. What is yours?
- My name is Fatma. We live on the street behind the park.
- We are very close too. It will be easy to meet.

Fatma was very happy to find someone to talk in Berlin. From that day on, families started to visit each other. Ali had been a good friend of Ulvi effendi the husband of Fevziye who introduced them to other families. Men were gathering at weekends and the women were getting together during the weekdays. Helga was mostly alone at home during day times when Ali was at work, Hasan was in school and Fatma was with her friends. She used to read books after finishing house hold work in those days. As a matter of fact she was a college graduate having forced to accept house hold service since there were no jobs available. Helga had not regretted taking the job.

Hasan was very clever and Fatma quite friendly. Ali was a contrast to all the stories she heard about the rude Ottoman men. He was an intellectual gentleman and a handsome young man like a God who came out from Greek mythology.

It was the laundry day and Helga was washing the linens. She did not hear Ali entered the room. She was kneeling in front of the bowl with stripped legs.

- How are you doing Helga? Are you washing the laundry?

Ali efendi had talked to her but preferred to watch. He wondered how he had not realized that she had such white legs and healthy breasts.

- Yes Ali. Fatma went to meet with her friends and I wanted to finish laundry before collecting Hasan. Why did you come so early today?
- Our lecturer could not attend today due to his illness. Students were let free.
- Would you like to eat something Ali?
- Thanks Helga. I stopped at a restaurant on the way home. Just make me a coffee when you finish.
- After I pour the water out of the bowl I will make your coffee.
- I better help you then if I wish to have my coffee soon.

Ali poured the water from the bowl. They discharged the wet linens to another bowl. In the meantime they both kneeled and got quite close to one another. Being so close to her golden hair and touching his legs to Helga's white legs had excited Ali efendi. Helga's heart started to beat stronger when her hands touched this young man's hands. She was secretly in love with him for a long time. Nothing could stop them and did not. Ali graduated in 1891 and they had been the most passionate lovers till last day.

Sultan Hamid had sent Ali's parents, Pakize hatun and Hamid aga to Berlin to witness the graduation ceremony of their son. As a matter of fact they felt an unforgettable pride by seeing that Ali had finished his school with the best achievement grade. They could never dream of loving their grandson Hasan so much. Their daughter-in-law Fatma was well adapted to a strange land but missed her parents and would be happy to return to Istanbul. Unfortunately her in-laws had brought unpleasant news that Ali had to stay for another year by the order of the Sultan, to complete his doctorate degree to lecture engineering in the university. They decided to take Fatma and Hasan with them to Istanbul and leave Ali alone in Berlin one more year. Fatma was not worried since she could entrust Ali to Helga who was supposed to meet all requirements of the young man.

During his last year in Berlin, Ali had enlarged his environment not only with academic circles but embassy members as well. One of them was the consulate secretary Hans Peter. He was frequently meeting Ali at home and had fallen in love with Helga whom at last proposed marriage. Helga had talked about it with Ali. They had together lived a great love and been unimaginably happy. But both were aware that it could not be continued and Helga had all the right to secure her future, to love her own baby. Ali had to leave Berlin next year and could not take Helga with him, neither did he wish to leave her alone without any support. They decided together that Helga should accept Hans Peter's proposal. They lived last time, a love matured by the past years but forced to separation in future. They promised not to see each other after this last union. But they could not keep their promises and have been several times together after Helga married to Hans Peter, till Ali left Berlin in 1892. At home Ali was called by sultan Hamid.

- Ali you made me so happy that it is impossible to define. Let me introduce you to Halet efendi, the director of the Istanbul technical university. He was complaining about having difficulty finding a lecturer for the school.

Halet efendi liked Ali after a short talk. They all agreed that Ali would start teaching in the university after fall.

The life of Ali after this appointment was very comfortable in Istanbul. His father gave him the upper floor of his mansion in Akaretler which was close to university. They were pleased to be at the same home with their grandson. Fatma was happy to be closer to her parents after so many years of separation. She could now raise her only son Hasan in her own country near her parents who loved him so much. The years passed quickly and Hasan came to the age to be the graduate of primary school. It was now the time to consider his future education.

not in the classes but in social activities. In such an activity Jenny met the love of her life. She saw Hasan in a get together party, near the desk of the bar. The tall, athletic boy was like a mythology figure of strength. A gravity of effection, pulled her near him uncontrollably. Hasan had seen and realized that the girl was coming near him willingly. He greeted herself and introduced himself without waiting. Jenny was at loss. She had heard Ottoman Empire stories but never met any Turk. Hasan was speaking English in American accent but behaving as an English gentleman. From that night on, they have been an inseparable couple.

In 1908, when Hasan was about to finish the second class of the law faculty, Jenny's father Mr. James decided to open an affiliate of his company in London. He came to England for this purpose. He visited Jenny in her school.

He then filed an application to open his company. After getting necessary permissions, the time had come to select the personnel for his Law firm. At this stage Jenny decided to introduce Hasan to her father. Meeting of the two most important men of her life, came out unexpectedly positive. Mr. Richard had so much appreciated Hasan that he offered him apprenticeship in his company during his free times and summer vacation. It was an unthinkable opportunity for a young law school student. Hasan accepted the offer right away and started to work in the firm, at off the school hours. Mr. Richard stayed one more month to see everything was smoothly progressing. He thought to take his daughter home when the schools would be closed for vacation. He watched Hasan carefully during this time and increasingly admired his capacity in solving the problems. Very close to his departure time, Jenny asked her father to work in the newly opened London branch in the summer. The old man had understood everything. His lazy and irresponsible daughter had fallen in love with Hasan and willing to work in the vacation just to be close to him. He questioned her.

- Jenny I want to ask you a private question. Do you have any affair with Hasan?
- Yes daddy I love him so much that I cannot think of a life without him.
- Hasan is really an adorable man. You know, how does he feel about you?
- He wants to marry me. I wanted to tell you this, after you met him. Do you approve our marriage daddy?
- I approve your relationship with all my heart Jenny. But I wish both of you to finish the school before marrying.

Jenny informed Hasan next day her conversation with her father. They were so happy that they could not wait any longer. They visited a jewelry shop and bought their engagement rings before a dinner appointment with Jenny's father. Their happiness continued until the last day of their life. In the spring time of 1910, Hasan and Jenny graduated from their schools. They went to New York to visit Jenny's parents where they officially married to continue their lives as husband and wife. They spent their honey moon mostly in New York with the parents. One month later they returned London to run their law firm. When their son Hakan was born in 1911 they were happier than ever.

6

GALLIPOLI SETLLEMENT OF HAMID AGA

Hamid aga, woke up on a hot summer morning in 1908, learned the declaration of 2nd lawfulness restoration. Two days ago he was together with the Sultan who had not told him anything. Of course the state affairs could not be spoken openly. He was still astonished. A messenger came to his room to inform the invitation of Sultan. When he went there, he saw Ali near Sultan. He was more curious.

- Hamid aga, have you heard the declaration of my 2nd lawfulness decree?
- Yes your majesty I heard. I hope it can be durable this time
- Do you guess what does it mean Ali efendi? That means they will soon dethrone me. After 32 years of a peaceful period in the country with no big territorial loss, there will again be unrest and riots in many corners of the Empire. Many territories will be lost for lack of prudence. Many

young men will die for the sake of fame. The tragedy is;

I am afraid that there will be no recovery this time and the Ottoman Empire will come to the end.

- What are you saying your majesty? God save all of us.
- If it had been my life at stake it would not be important. Don't you remember how many valuable men I have killed for unattainable dreams? I understand now I executed them for nothing. In a short time no one will appreciate my sacrifices for the integrity of the Empire. But you, Hamid aga and Ali efendi, are not ungrateful. I therefore want to do a favor to you, while I have still power.
- Your majesty you already did us the greatest favors, we would not expect from the closest families.
- Listen to me Hamid aga. Immediately, as of today, I want you and your son to leave Istanbul cutting off all your ties. Hamid I know it will be difficult for you to separate from the city of your ancestors. Ali efendi it may come strange to you why I want you to leave the university after I spent so much efforts on your education. But I am still insistent on your leaving both, for your own well-being.

- Your majesty I have graduated from Robert College and studied in Germany only by your generosity. My son Hasan is in London now only because of you. If you tell me to leave Istanbul now, I'll do it without asking and hesitation.
- You will soon learn it Ali efendi. Not only you but everybody in the Empire will see it. But I do not want to leave you hopeless after I passed away. I donate you, four villages in Gallipoli, from my own estate. Two of them are on the coast and active in wheat and rice plantation. In the others two on the hill, there are cattle breeding and dairy farms. Go there to have a happy and safe life with your children. Tell Hasan not to come to Istanbul till sun rises again over our land. This is a purse full of gold for your moving and settlement. Money did not help to me, let it be useful to you. Unfortunately Hamid aga and Pakize hatun did not live too long after they moved Gallipoli. Ali efendi owned the four villages alone.

7

DETHRONEMENT
OF SULTAN

On 24th July 1908, second lawfulness decree was declared but the things got worsened. On July 31 Tobacco workers went on strike. On August 28 and September 15 railway workers followed. The people, provoked by young Turks, were screaming for war. Parliament gathered on December 17th. 1908. But no action could be taken to calm down the public. On March 20th 1909 custom workers went on strike. Hasan Fehmi from freedom newspaper, was killed on April 6th Conservatives uplifted in a revolt on April 13th. Parliament decided dethrone sultan Hamid on April 27th they sent him to Salonica and replaced the exiled sultan by Mehmet Reshad. By this move, Union and Progress party leaders (young Turks) became the undisputed power of the country. They were discussing their future moves.

- We acted correctly by dethroning Abdulhamid. His successor sultan Reshad is a manageable man.

- By this way, we had the opportunity to progress the country by acting hand in hand. We shall make decisions by unity. None of us will claim leadership and always inform the others for any action.
- Ottoman Empire got weaker by years. The main reason of this decline was non-Muslim minorities. We should therefore punctuate our Muslim identity.
- You are wrong my friends. What brought the Ottomans so many years together was the attitude of non-ethnic and non-religious policies. If we discriminate now, shall we not upset our subjects in Balkans? Shall we not be losing many strategic territories in Europe? Will there not be up-rises of Bulgarians, Rumanians, Macedonians and Greeks? Can they not declare independence?
- Mustafa, we shall not be able to hold them together anyway. Religion is an important factor to hold the communities together.
- That is the main reason why we should not discriminate humans by race and religion. Just the contrary, we should even cancel religious schools and courts, just it is in secular European countries. We should even equalize men and women rights to the contrary to the Islam teachings.
- I am in favor of giving good education to our women as well. But they should not pretend the

European women by losing Muslim identity. We shall then not be recognized as the caliph of the Muslim world and weakening.

- I recall you once more. Have we not dethroned the sultan for freedom? What logic is there to continue the sultanate?

- Sultanate is needed to continue the caliphate. We may not defend our lands in Europe against the Christians. But in Egypt and Middle East at least we can beat the British Empire by the cooperation of our Muslim brothers.

- Is caliphate needed then to prove our statesmanship? With what human sources and technical superiority we'll beat the British Empire? Why should we not be ally with them?

- You forget Mustafa, technical superiority of our German allies. Have they not constructed Istanbul Hejaz railway? Can they not provide all the ammunition needs of our army? Will great Turkish nation not sacrifice her sons for the sake of fame? Are there not our Muslim brothers in those countries Britain occupied? Will they not help the Caliph of Islam?

- Gentlemen, if you are going to be offensive, do it relying your own sources, not depending on technical superiority of Germans, nor the sacrifice of the young generation for the sake of your fame. Let me tell you the cruel truth. In case of a fight Arabs will take part on the strong side like who has the British pound,

8

GALLIPOLI DAYS OF ALI EFENDI

Ali efendi was living a heavenly life in Gallipoli. It was like a dream, to watch the trees in different colors, collect fruits in all seasons, breed the cattle and milk them to produce the famous Thrace white cheese. It was also a fun for him to walk on the muddy soil together with workers and throw seed on the rice fields. But his greatest pleasure was to go out fishing. He was getting on boat with his men to lay down their nets before sun rise. After pulling up the nets he was curious in collecting the catches of the day to select the best ones for home. His father was the chief cook in the palace but had never tasted delicious fish as freshly caught red sea bream. Still they use to catch his favorite fish in the nights with torches. Sardines were small in size but very rich in healthy and tasty oil content. Native people used to grill sardines wrapping them with grape leaves.

In the first year however Ali efendi was busier with construction. He first built a sea front house for the family, at a size and comfort never seen before. There was a slide on the shore, to launch down and pull out the boats. The house was inside of a garden and there were all kind of trees and flowers between the shore and their house. It was not only the house, Ali efendi spent time to build. He brought samples from Switzerland and put some conical chimneys on the milk boilers at the dairy. There were some hooks, where the smoke was going out from the chimney, to hang some fish and meat pieces to be dried while the cheese production proceeded. He also made some conditioning chambers to dry the cheeses scientifically instead of letting them dry in open air. The folds for sheep and cattle were modernized to provide utmost hygienic conditions. Animals were no longer eating or drinking polluted stuff. He even hired physicians for veterinary care to fight and cure the disease. These actions did not only increase his earnings but served as an example to the villagers whose respect for him was growing.

Soon the villagers started to call him Ali aga. (Master Ali)

When he was sitting on a couch in his garden after a tiring working day, in the evenings or nights, he was dreaming his days in Germany and mostly about his affair with Helga. He had to leave Helga but he could not forget her. He was getting letters from her two three times a year. But he read them hundred times. He was now 48 but not old enough to forget a passionate love. Besides, clean air and agricultural activities had made him healthier than ever.

Unfortunately the relations between him and his wife was getting colder by each passing day. Cultural adaptation problems with wife Fatma, had become evident in Berlin but grown wider in Gallipoli. How active Ali efendi is, that much passive Fatma was. She had devoted herself to religious retirement without realizing the dissatisfaction of her gesture on Ali efendi.

Sultan Hamid's predictions were coming true one by one. The war, in Balkans, Middle East, Caucasus and North Africa, was about to burst out leaving the Istanbul people unsure of their next day. Young men were summoned military to fight and possibly die in far frontiers. Ali efendi had no worry for the future and always been grateful to the sultan. That day he was on the way to dairy enjoying the beauties of the spring time. He saw cattle pasturing on the meadows being tended by young boys. Getting closer to the folds he saw women kneeled near the cows to milk them. One of them attracted the attention of Ali efendi with her yellow hairs poured on her shoulders. He recalled the day he made love with Helga. He was missing those days so much that he could not leave the spot. At last she filled the cattle and stood up to carry the milk to the dairy. She saw the well-respected owner of the farms.

- How are you Ali aga? I did not know you were here.
- I came to see how things were going in the dairy.
- Everything is abundant this year. Look at the milk, I took from yellow cow. The kettle is almost full.

She had difficulty in carrying the kettle. Ali aga asked her.

- Where are you going to take the kettle sister?
- I shall go the cheese factory far ahead.
- Let me help you. What is your name?
- My name is Zeynep, Ali aga.
- How long have you been working here Zeynep?
- I started the job after my husband passed away.
- Do you have any children sister?
- No Ali aga I do not have.
- Where are you living now?
- I am the daughter of alderman Salim efendi. I used to live here when my husband was alive. I am still here.

On the way to the cheese factory, Ali ağa and Zeynep saw some newly born white lambs. Zeynep screamed.

- Look at those new lambs Ali aga. How beautiful they are.
- Would you like to pet them Zeynep?
- We believe to pet a white lamb brings good luck.

Ali aga shouted the sheep tender.

- Hey young man. Can you bring me a white lamb?

Sheep tender got excited when saw Ali aga. He ran to catch a lamb and brought it to Aga. In the meantime little lamb was bleating to call the mother. As a matter of fact a big sheep followed the tender. Zeynep took the lamb in her arms. She sat on a rock and kissed the animal. In the meantime Ali aga looked the mother sheep. Asked the boy

- What is your name young man?
- My name is Mestan, Ali aga.
- Tell me Mestan. Were many lambs born this year?
- It is a year of abundance Ali aga. We don't have too many lambs right now. But look at the sheep. They will all have babies in a short time.

They left the lamb and walked to the cheese factory. Fruit trees were colorful in blossoming flowers. Red poppies and white daisies popped up their heads on the fields. Zeynep was trying to collect and put them in a pocket on her skirt.

- Zeynep what are you going to do with those flowers?
- We make poppy syrup and drink it during the spring time. We believe it can give us health and strength. Daisies we dry and drink all year long against cold.
- I need both those healings Zeynep. Tell you what, after taking the kettle to the factory we come here with two sacks and collect healing flowers. You then make me the syrup and dry the daisies.
- The way you like it Ali aga.

    At the factory gate master Recai met them. Ali aga asked.

- How things are going, master Recai?
- God save you Ali aga. With the new technics you taught us our production increased considerably in better quality.
- I liked it. What are you going to do now?
- We shall strain cheese from the boiling milk Ali aga. If you wish, sit on this chair and watch. I can then prepare a breakfast for you, all made of our own production of milk, cream, cheese, yoghurt and jar.
- Thank you Recai. Would you like to join me sister Zeynep?

Zeynep embarrassed with the proposal. In their traditions women and children could not sit together with men. Ali aga felt her hesitation and explained.

- Master Recai. I met sister Zeynep while milking the cow. On the way to dairy she explained me how do you make poppy syrup and dry the daisies to make tea. If you give us two sacks, she will collect flowers while I watch pasturing of the cattle.

Villagers got use to Ali aga who was interested in every detail of the work to solve their problems. Their earnings increased after Ali aga, whom therefore was respected by all. On the way to Zeynep's house they had collected plenty of flowers. Zeynep introduced Ali aga, to her father Salim efendi and mother Kadriye hatun. While drinking coffee Ali aga asked.

- I was walking through the folds, I met sister Zeynep who told me that you make poppy syrup good for health Salim efendi. I feel tired in the spring. Do you think it helps me?
- We benefit a lot Ali aga. I hope it helps you too.
- O.K. when can you make it ready?
- In one week time, it will be ready.
- Is it true Salim efendi? Does it take so long?

- To prepare the syrup takes one hour. To mature the syrup under sun, takes one week.
- O.K. then. I will disturb you a week later to get my syrup.
- You will never disturb us, but always honor us. Next week is our spring festival called Hidirellez here. If you come early in the morning you join the festivities. We shall then be honored if you have lunch with us.
- O.K. Salim efendi. Next week at seven. Is it alright?
- Very much so Ali aga.

Ali aga could hardly wait for a week. He was not interested in dethronement of sultan, nor with his successor. In his world at Gallipoli there were no place for ugliness, unloyalty and disliked surprises. In this land the people used to wait new born lambs, flowering meadows and listen to singing nightingales in the spring. Summer was the time of golden grains on the fields, maturing fruits on the trees and vegetables in the gardens. The autumn would be the harvesting time of everything on the fields and in the sea. The heart of the villagers were as clean as forest air. Their behavior were as pure as spring waters.

Ali aga arrived village on May 6 at seven o'clock in the morning. Villagers had gathered in front of the alderman's house. Salim efendi welcomed Ali aga. When they all sat under the trellis, those villagers who had a wish, came close to the village writer who was a must when most of the population was illiterate. He wrote all wishes on a piece of paper. He gave these papers to the concerned villagers who were hanging them under the branches of rose trees.

They believed two holy people, one came from the sea the other from land, would meet under a rose tree on May 6, to make every wish come true. A big fire was lit. People jumped on it to get rid of all troubles.

Ali aga pretended the villagers and jumped on fire few times, among the big noise of applauds. Then villagers came close to the village writer and drew the fortune telling papers prepared before. Village writer was reading them loudly after each draw. Ali aga followed the villagers and gave his paper to the writer for reading.

"You don't laugh on festive day
You don't know what you will say
Don't try to mislead us
You're in love in secret way"

The villagers heard the fortune and laughingly shouted

"Ali aga, tell us your problem."

They sat on the breakfast table together with their beloved aga who listened them one by one. He gave instant orders to the responsible people to solve some of the problems. Everybody was happy with Hidirellez festivity.

After the villagers departed Ali and Salim agas stayed alone while sipping their coffee. Salim aga thanked.

- We have been very pleased with your visit Ali aga. No one have ever done this. I hope all your wishes come true.
- I hope so Salim aga. I have been very pleased to be with you. Gallipoli revived me. I feel like I was reborn. My only trouble is having some problems with my wife Fatma. I like active life as to go fishing in the mornings, to work in the field's afternoon and visit folds and dairy in the evenings. She closed herself in the house in full seclusion.
- Ali aga how nice you speak. Many hodjas visited our village mosque and each recommended different thing to be close to the Lord. I sometimes think, instead of listening to the contrasting words of clerics, would it not be better if we had followed the voice of our heart? I do not know reading but if I had known I would read holy books myself.

I still prefer to learn the religion from someone like you instead of listening to old people. We loved you so much Ali aga. We found you near us, whenever we needed. We would love to solve your problem. I did not meet your wife. May be she is tired to adapt herself to your life style. Why don't you marry to a younger woman then? That is the way we do it here. If you like we can even look one for you.

- You got me quite correctly Salim aga. Do you really mean to find a young woman for me?
- I do everything for you Ali aga.
- Do you give me your daughter Zeynep for instance?

Salim aga was not prepared for such a question. He still answered in an unhesitant manner.

- Zeynep is a thirty years old widow. Who can she find, better than you?
- Look Salim aga. Thank you for accepting me as your son-in-law. But I do not want your consent alone if Zeynep does not want me.
- Don't worry Ali aga. I shall talk both her and my wife to answer you next week.

When Ali aga told his decision to Fatma, she was upset.

- I would not expect this from you Ali. At least you should have informed me before deciding. I think I have the right to expect that much courtesy from you being the mother of your only son.

I know, I could have no word to object if you had told me but you would not be breaking my heart Ali.

Fatma hatun, after separation from her son was now facing the loss of her husband. She knew that she had neglected earthly life to reach a promised after life. Was the world so much worthless to retire? She might have regretted if she had a choice. But she was aware of being too late now.

Shortly after this talk Ali aga got married to Zeynep in 1909.

He had once more found the happy days he passed with Helga. His life was more colorful now and he had more hopes for the future. The birth of his son Husein in 1910, multiplied his happiness. He had missed the experience of fatherly love. Salim aga was happy too. When his widowed daughter Zeynep had lost her hopes to remarry, she had found the richest man of the district. She would not have any trouble in all her life. On top of everything they had grandson Husein now. Fatma was at loss at the beginning. But later she loved little Husein as hers. She appreciated Zeynep too for her courtesy and friendship who had taken over all housework from her. Fatma devoted herself fully to religious retirement. Her only wish now was pilgrimage.

9

BALKAN WAR

Young Turks had no achievement in the country and messed up everything in Balkans. They were defending pan-islamist policy on one side and freedom on the other. At the end of this turmoil; Montenegron, Bulgarian, Serbian and Greek nationalities brought their forces together in October 18, 1912 and started Balkan war with the support of Italy, France and Britain. Union & Progress party leaders had not only lost in Balkans but in Libya too. They met in Istanbul after all these defeats

- We were seriously defeated friends not in Balkans but in North Africa as well.
- Sometimes I wonder pasha, why we dethroned sultan Hamid who had not lost major territory during his reign of 33 years. Look at us. What we did in 3 years?
- Don't be demoralized my friends. We did all these things because of our patriotism. West Thrace could not be held together any way. If we reestablish our country on the basis of Muslim brotherhood we'll be stronger and richer.

- Had a country patriots like us, she would not need enemy. If our dreams on Muslim brotherhood, come out like our other plans, it will be a great pity for the country.
- Why do you speak so? Look at Istanbul-Hejaz railway system. It works perfectly. That means we can send troops very easily Egypt to regain our prestige. Don't forget Egypt is still under our reign and the very important Suez Canal is there. Richest oil reserves are in Mesopotamia. If we can act together with Germans, we can give a good lesson to the British Empire.
- Instead of chasing after lecturing others, why don't we try to learn our lessons? You explained Balkan defeat with Islam, what do you say about Libya then? Did we not have Muslim brothers in that country to help us to be victorious? If in the Middle East our brothers act like the Libyans what shall we do?
- We lost there for not having shipped ammunition. It won't be the same in the Middle East with the railway system.
- Pasha when we claimed the administration of the country, we promised honesty but we lie constantly and cheat the public. The bribery rumors roared up not only in Istanbul but in the Middle East as well. We hear that many of the Arab tribes are sold for pound. Why can we not prevent this and stop inefficiency.

- We do all our best. But we should remember the Byzantine way of accusations. Those who have nothing to promise, blame their opponents.
- O.K. pasha what are we promising for the future, except our attempts to regain our lost prestige?
- Our promise is to take part on the correct side of Europe, quickly falling apart and not to leave oil reserves to Britain.
- What are we doing friends, is gambling with the fate of the country. We bet all our wealth on one country. We do not think what we'll do if our partner loses. Assume you proved right, we won oil rich territories. Do we have technology to exploit reserves? Does even Germany have that knowhow?

Why don't we then come to agreement with Britain before not to risk the future of the country, neither the lives of the young generations?

- Pasha you have not understood one thing. Young Turkish men do not hesitate to sacrifice their lives for their country.
- Because incapable military officers always cheated young men with lies appealing to their patriotic feelings to send them to death, to throw their country to disaster, just to satisfy their ambitious dreams and search for fame.

10

OTTOMAN EMPIRE ENTERS WORLD WAR I

After the assassination of archduke Ferdinand in Sarajevo, the Austria-Hungary Empire declared war against Serbia. This way, a long awaited fire was sparked. In the meantime Ottoman general Enver, married Naciye hatun, the niece of the Sultan. With this marriage Enver became the son-in-law of the imperial dynasty and was promoted to Chief of the Staff position.

Union & progress party leaders are in a meeting.

- I am afraid the assassination of prince Ferdinand of Austria will trigger the war in Europe. Thanks god that we shall be neutral this time. We made an agreement with Great Britain to train our army and by ordering two war ships to them we reconciled our conflicts. We are also on good terms with Germany after the construction of Hejaz-Baghdad railway system. Let us not mess up with the war and stay away this time not to risk the country.

- Why do you say so my friend? If we are going to follow the passive policies of Sultan Hamid, why did we dethrone him? We are here to bring the Ottomans to their former glorious days.
- You may appreciate starting new deals with the British Empire but our Chief of staff made a secret agreement with Germans. Britain learned this and stopped manufacturing our warships, they are not going to deliver them, although we paid the price in cash.

Some of the party members are furious and ask resignation of the pasha. He takes the word.

- I agree, my mistake friends, and resigning is not important for me. But if we resign now there will be a vacuum in the administration and that will please our enemies who refuse to deliver the warships for which we paid in cash. I made a mistake by paying cash for the warships but I also corrected my mistake; In a short time our German friends agreed to deliver us two warships greater than what we would get from English manufactures.

In fact Germany delivered two warships and Turkish flags were hung on Yavuz and Midilli. Before the Turkish officers got on board they sailed out to the Black Sea under German commandment to bomb the Russian ports and one of them was sunk in the black sea by the Russian navy. The cost of this event was very heavy. Allies comprised of Great Britain, France and Russia gave an ultimatum on August 18, 1914. When they could not get a satisfactory answer Ottoman Empire found itself in the World War I, on October 31, 1914. The party members are on discussions

- Congratulations pasha. At last you succeeded to throw the country to an unnecessary adventure.
- I have not done anything. We did everything together.
- How do you speak like this? You have not informed us anything. At least let us keep away any adventure after this.
- That's impossible. Before the war started, we sent troops of 70.000 soldiers to regain the lost territory in Caucasus. Did we not pasha?
- Exactly my friend. Before giving the lessons to British Empire, would it not be proper to reconcile our conflict with Russia in Caucasus?
- What do we hear pasha. When we founded this party, did we no say to be a union? There is no logic to send young men to Caucasus before the winter. How shall we provide their need on snowy mountains?
- We shipped their needs by vessels from black sea. They are all heroes. They will win the war

with their bayonets even if they cannot get any ammunition.

- Pasha, don't try to find excuses for your mistakes. Soldiers can fight against the enemy but not against the cold as Napoleon's soldiers could not do, in the Russian steps in the winter. They will perish without even firing their guns. You are worse than the cruelest murderer, who would kill few but not 70.000. Why did you not inform us?

- I sent them without informing you because I am the chief commander of staff. I decided so before confronting Britain in the Middle East, Caucasus should have been solved.

- If we fail in Caucasus shall we not be weaker for the next? Families do not grow their sons to be sacrificed in vain by the incompetent military commanders for unreal dreams. Why didn't you send your sons? Are they not Turks and Ottoman citizens?

- Pasha you go too far. You either be with us or go. Those have no courage cannot win anything.

- But cannot lose either. If the homeland is at risk then courage is a merit. If not, to start a war or enter it, is murder and the greatest betrayal of all.

- No one has right to suspect our honesty and patriotism.

- I prefer to deal with the clever of the enemy rather than the stupid of the honest. I can no more be part of your acts. I leave you right away.

Coming to your honesty, I hope you stay honest to resign quickly, when things go wrong.

The ships taking ammunition to Sarikamish are bombed and sunk in black sea. 70.000 soldiers die on Caucasus.

The committee is in the meeting again.

- Friends we experienced an unexpected disaster on eastern border. 70.000 soldiers became martyrs for their country.
- What are you talking pasha? How can they be martyr without firing a gun? They are the victims of our search for fame. One of our friends had warned this failure and asked us to be honest when things went wrong in last meeting. You know what? He has disappeared with no trace. During sultan Hamid times the people were being executed but not disappeared as happens now. Unfortunately it is too late to go back and find another sultan Hamid to bring integrity.
- Was it bad to make a military coup d'état?
- In our history all military coup d'états proved to be very bad. It is worse this time as we lost half of our country. It will be the same in the future as well. Because the main duty of the armed forces is not to turn the guns on their citizens and rulers, instead of the enemies. Only the stupid army commanders can believe the stories that

by changing the people they could improve the country.

- I wish to disappear too, instead of sharing your mistakes.
- Don't worry friends everything has been planned. We have 65.000 soldiers under the command of Zeki pasha in Palestine. I ordered them to attack British forces. We shall save Egypt from Britain with the help of our brothers.
- Why have we called ourselves a union? We have been founded by the intention to decide unanimously. You make decisions from which none of us is informed. May God damn us.

It happened so. Turkish forces confronted the British army on February 2, 1915. in Ismailiyah. In the meantime a sand storm delayed Turks for one day. British officers drove the Anzac and Indian forces on the Turks, when the storm stopped on February 3. The fate of the Ottomans was once more a tragic collapse.

11

BRITISH EMPIRE DESIGNS FOR OTTOMANS

After the Ottoman attack in Egypt on February 3 1915, British cabinet is in the meeting to debate the situation.

- Gentlemen we have escaped from the surprise attack of Turks by great luck. We cannot rely on luck next time as to have a sand storm. We should therefore find a solution for keeping them away from Egypt.
- The only solution to keep the Turks and Germans away from Egypt is to open a new frontier. In such a place that they can not even think of Egypt.
- Can our admiralty minister clarify what he means?
- I of course mean to target the place where their brain and heart is located. We have not delivered their warships. One of the two ships manufactured by Germans for them, was sunk by Russians. Under these conditions we can

pass our navy through Dardanelles. They will be paralyzed, and will not be able to think about Egypt when they see the British navy on the shores of Istanbul.

- Do you think our navy is sufficient to do this?
- It may or may not be. We shall not do this alone. We shall ask the cooperation of France.
- Assume we do this to keep Turks away from Egypt. What will be the benefit for the French Government?
- French people will join us, to prove their superiority over Germans. Moreover we can promise them some low oil reserve area like Syria. In the meantime, we secretly made an agreement with the emir of Hejaz who will give us soldiers against the freedom of Palestine and Mecca.
- But, have we not decided to give Palestine to Jews?
- This is called diplomacy my friend. Let us first bring him to our side then we come to agreement against some oil shares. In the meantime our agents succeeded to revolt Arabs against Turks in Yemen. Emir of Gazza will also support us in Palestine.

The plans of Admiralty minister proved to be wrong. Combined British French navy forces were defeated in the Dardanelles.

- Winston, my friend. What you said would be easy, came out very hard. We could not pass through the strait.
- Unfortunately we couldn't. We did not think they would lay mines on the water.
- We had planned to demoralize Turks. Contrary they found moral with our defeat.
- At no cost we can give up our plans to defeat Ottomans in securing Suez Canal and lands having rich oil reserves.
- Gallipoli my friends? If we could not pass Dardanelles by our navy then we land to Gallipoli which is a 100 miles long peninsula and no one can predict our exact landing point.
- That really seems doable. Only there is one problem. Our main army is in Europe at war now. If we shift part of our military forces than we shall be weak in Europe.
- My dear Prime minister. I did not mean to use noble British soldiers in Gallipoli landing. We shall mostly call Australian aborigines and New Zealand Maoris. If we mix them with some Indian soldiers and French one for fame, here is a perfect landing army. Of course commanders will be British.
- You are very clever Winston. We recently recognized the independence of Australia and New Zealand. They are eager to prove the pride of being a nation by joining an operation of success. Do you all approve Gallipoli landing?

- Of course we do. But if we defeat the Turks, how we shall keep such a big area like Anatolia under control?
- It is easy gentlemen. We let the Greeks occupy west Anatolia and the Armenians east. Than we shall use them as guards.

12

GALLIPOLI
LANDING

On 25 April 1915, the British navy arrives at Gallipoli. Landing starts at dawn. After few hours officers are in discussion.

- My dear Admiral. Unfortunately landing does not proceed successfully, as we hoped. Machine gun fires, from the opposite hills, killed 2000 of our soldiers even before setting foot on ground. We thought to surprise Turks with our landing point and we found them waiting for us at just this spot in big trenches.
- We shall bomb those hills after sun rise to make it easy.
- I am afraid it will not help either. Because Turks dug deep trenches on the other side of the hills which we cannot see to bomb. As a matter of fact our landing spot has been wrong sir. Look at the hills after the beach. Our soldiers will have to climb if they can set foot on the beach. There is a beach two miles south of this spot where there

is no hill to hide for Turks and no barrier for our soldiers to climb.

- What do you say colonel? If we change the landing spot after operation started, how can we explain it to Admiralty in London? Shall we say excuse us we made a mistake?
- But if we continue operation from this spot, we shall have much more casualties. Is it not pity to these young men?
- When we collected them in Australia and New Zealand we did not tell them it would be easy? Victory needs sacrifices.
- I do not want to be disrespectful to you sir, but I feel responsibility for their lives. They were raised by their families with great efforts. They entrusted them to us to honor their country. What would happen if they knew that we cheated them? We sent them to death not to honor our country but just to save our prestige.
- When you will be promoted to my rank colonel you will see that I was correct. When Napoleon or Hitler ordered their army to march on Russia did they do something different?

I order you colonel to forget all your words. Your duty now is to encourage your soldiers to attack tomorrow.

Next day the colonel carries out what he is ordered to do.

- Australian, New Zealand, Indian, British and French heroes. We have not been successful with our first landing attempt. Because cruel Turks trapped us. But today will be very different. Our navy will first bomb all Turkish trenches where machine guns are hidden. You will then attack like a lightning and win the battle.
- My colonel. I talk on behalf of my friends as well. Why we are here? What is the purpose of Gallipoli landing?
- That is a very good question lieutenant. What we want to achieve here is to destroy the greatest enemy of Britain. They are barrier in front of us to run Suez Canal to exploit oil reserves in Middle East.
- Yes sir. Were Egypt and Middle East not under their reign over the centuries? Why don't we come to agreement to save the lives of so many young men?
- You are right lieutenant. Do you think we did not want to?

But each time we tried, they refused us to the contrary of our Arab friends. Our enemy Turks are irreconcilable and we want to save humanity from them. You have the great opportunity now to eliminate human enemies. Chris, will help us in our holy battle.

13

HASAN'S FAMILY ON THE WAY TO USA

On May 6, 1915 Hasan received a letter from his wife Jenny dated April 25, from London.

"My only love Hasan. Today is the seventh month of our separation. Remember we had decided to move to the USA on October 1, 1914. You wished to see your family for one last time and went Turkey. I will remember that day as the worst time of my life. All disasters of the world came one upon another after that day. Britain and Turkey joined the war on separate sides. After that moment I have not lived a happy day. Even our only son Hakan did not give me consolation. Because I saw you, in his eyes and in all his manners. I know he has missed you as much as me. He comes to my bed in the nights and tell me the stories about your return. But can anybody in the world replace you?

My London life has been an ordeal for me. In the university, in the company, in friendly reunions everything reminds me of you. We were not two sweethearts. We were one soul in two different bodies. I missed you so much I would gladly give half of my life to be with you. But by each passing day my hopes are diminishing, my love. I received a letter, last week from my father. He immediately calls me to take over the office, since doctors predict that he has maximum one year time left. His invitation sounded logical to accept since that was our plan. Besides no one is sure the future of Britain under the continuing German bombs. I want our son to live in a peaceful world with no wind of separation. We cannot continue our happiness in a world of hatred. I wish him a life with no worry. I hope one day you will join us to complete our happiness and make us live in heaven. With all these thoughts I decided to wait you in New York, instead of risking our lives in London. In the meantime I saw an ad from German officers declaring that two countries were in war and all vessels would be bombed around British Isles. I was again hopeless and indecisive that I saw another add. Cunard maritime company was informing the Liverpool - New York voyage of their super cruiser Lusitania which crossed the Atlantic 101 times so far at a speed of 25 miles without any risk, as their cruise liner was 10 miles faster than German submarines. In short my love I reserved our place with Hakan to sail out on May 6. I'll write you as soon as we arrive New York. Jenny"

After sending the letter to Hasan she worked very hard to liquidate her responsibilities in London. She assigned the barristers who would run the law office after herself. She found a new tenant for her house. She invited all her friends to her home before leaving. They were all envying her, because of getting away from hell. She arrived to Liverpool one day earlier on May 5, with her son Hakan. She watched the ship at port. She could not dream of such a magnificent thing. With four chimneys on the board, Lusitania was like a small village. She felt more confident in God. If the lord made this miracle possible for her. Lord would certainly do it for Hasan who had been similarly hopeful by receiving the letter from Jenny. He dreamed of happy days with his wife and son once he could arrive New York. He had regretted to come Gallipoli where his father had married a young woman from whom had a son. His mother was half insane. If he could meet Jenny and son, none of his parents would be important.

In the meantime Cunard representatives were in touch with admiralty officers.

- Our Lusitania cruiser will sail out to New York on May 6, with 702 crews and 1257 passengers. We learned some German submarines were seen around the isles. Can you give us escort until leaving the dangerous waters.

- You ask favoritism from us. If we do it for you what will the other ship owners say?
- We don't think that on any other ship, 2000 lives are at risk. Are they?
- No they are not. But we don't think any of those ships, cruise faster than you. With a speed 10 miles faster than German submarines you have more chance to escape.
- You mean you will not give escort to us?
- No we don't. We only say we shall look for availability. We heard that some cruise liners are not sailing at full speed to save coal. Don't do this till you reach the safe waters.
- We already gave the instruction. You think a company at our size will do such a stupidity?
- We have agreed then. We shall do our best to escort you.

Sometime later this communication, German officers on a submarine in Irish waters are chatting among themselves.

- Our fuel is running short colonel. Would it not be good to go back Germany after yesterday hunt?
- Do you call it hunt, Hans? We learned that she was a vessel slightly bigger than a fishing boat called Earl of Lathom. You are still right. We should soon sail back to Wilhelmshaven. But there is a heavy fog now. As soon as it clears we shall be on our way back.

- Colonel, at least we should take a route farther than the coast not to be caught by escorts.
- But this time our fuel my not take us to our destination.
- Colonel, our periscope officer informs that a British cargo ship is on our route.
- Let me see. This is a small 6000 ton vessel. There are poor sailors in these ships who work to look after their families. Go up to surface and make warning shots to give time to the sailors to leave the ship and rescue themselves.
- They all got on boats. Shall we send the torpedo?
- Yes we shall, to sink our first target at 7.40 in the morning.

They had only three torpedoes on hand which had to be kept to defend themselves on the return way as per the rules.

Jenny and Hakan got on board on May 6, 1915. Their cabin was on the upper floor of the right side very close to rear flag. They walked on the board until departure time. Not only Jenny but Hakan liked the ship with play grounds, swimming pools, entertainment theatre and casino.

Lusitania was leaving Liverpool port. After passing Irish channel in short time they would be in the open seas and cruise in safer water. It was noon time after departure. Everybody rushed to restaurants. Hakan slept after lunch.

Jenny looked for safety belts in the shelves. She could not find any belt. She asked the waiter to bring one for her and one for Hakan. They were now sailing on risky waters. She wore herself and when Hakan woke up she helped him to wear. They could not go to restaurant with safety belts. So Jenny ordered dinner and the next morning breakfast to be brought to the room until they would be out of the risky area. When they fell asleep Lusitania was getting wireless messages.

- Hi captain we learned that German submarines torpedoed two ships. Admiralty asks you to cruise at high speed.
- It is too foggy now and we cannot cruise at high speed.
- If you cannot then sail in zig zags.

On May 7, in the morning the crew in a German submarine informed the steering chamber.

- Hi Captain, there is a huge cruise liner in front of us with four chimneys.
- If she has four chimneys it is Lusitania of the Cunard lines.
- Captain there are 2000 crews and passengers on the ship. Should we make warning shots on the surface?
- Unfortunately we can't do it this time. If we go up surface they see us and because they are faster

than us, they can escape. On the other hand we could be criticized for sinking Lusitania by our commanders. I therefore order you not to know that we hit Lusitania. Now send one torpedo to the spot, where the ship would be 20 seconds later.

In the meantime the sailor on the observation tower of the Lusitania saw the in-coming torpedo, shouted to the captain's cabin.

- There is a torpedo coming toward us from the right side.
- In the ships like Lusitania, if it is early observed and action taken, there was chance to escape, as there was plenty of time to change the route. Captain was not in his cabin pitily. Torpedo hit the ship somewhere between first and second chimneys. It was such a blast at 2.10 PM that nobody walking on the board could stay on foot. The ship bended in a few minutes to the right side which was the greatest luck of Jenny. Since the rescue boats on the left side could not be launched on to the water because of escalation. Jenny and Hakan were about to fall noon time sleep with their safety belts put on. Jenny took Hasan in her arms. Crew was taking first ladies and little children. So Jenny and Hasan easily found their way to the boat. Many passengers on the line were pushing each other. One crew

loosened the ropes and Jenny felt that their boat strongly hit on the water. Some passengers fell on water with this sudden strike. But Jenny and Hakan were on the narrow front side of the boat and firmly grabbed the sides of the boat. Some of those fell in the sea did not know to swim. Few of them could be held and taken into the boat. The others drowned before the eyes of others, among the screams.

The weather was clear. Kinsale and Queenstown coasts were 12 and 25 miles away. They immediately sent their rescue boats. Those who could swim and find seats in the boats saved their lives. Jenny and Hakan were among them. Unfortunately 1200 people died by drowning.

When the passengers set foot on island's ground, there were ambulance boats waiting. The passengers who did not need medical care were chatting among themselves.

- You know coast guard did not send escort although Cunard line asked for.
- What I heard that admiralty has not informed Cunard lines about sinking ships in the area.
- You know guys. I was on the board when one crew saw the coming torpedo and shouted to the steering cabin. But Captain was not there.
- Because he was with me in the casino.

- Should he not be in cabin while cruising on risky waters?
- Of course he should. Had he been in the cabin, he could even have saved the ship.
- According to the rules, Lusitania should have sailed at full speed in zig zags. None were observed by our captain.
- Let me tell you the most interesting thing. You know the captain is alive after hundreds of passengers died. Could it not be a British trick to enforce USA to enter the war?

In the meantime American consulate in Queenstown had sent the consulate officers, who hospitalized American citizens in need. They have been hosted few nights till another ship to New York was found. At last Jenny and Hakan arrived New York one week later than scheduled.

14

MARTYRDOM OF HASAN

Few weeks after Anzacs arrived Gallipoli, they realized how much lies they have been told about the cruelty, rudity and infidelity of Turks, just to attract young men to the military.

One of them was John White who expressed his feelings to his sweetheart in his letter.

"My love Becky. When military officers promoted us to join the army they had told us that our homeland needed patriotic young men to secure the interests of Australia and Britain in Egypt, Suez and Middle East. The future of our children would be darkened if we had not sacrificed our lives now. Do you remember one night we met at moon light on Bondi beach? You, me, our school mates Tom, Bill, neighbors Mary and Kevin were all together. You told us proudly that your brother Jerry had also joined army. You encouraged us to follow Jerry to fight against coward Turks and we all did it. From the very first days we landed here we understood that all were lies. How could Turks be coward that they are marching on bullets with bare chests? One night we had too many fallen comrades to take back to the trenches and we were too few to carry them. Guess what? Some Turks came out from their trenches and offered us help to carry our friends some of whom were badly in need of fresh water which was our main lacking. Observing our problem, a lieutenant brought plenty water in big jugs and clean bandages to help our injured friends.

None of their acts were the indications of cruelty. In reciprocate their gesture, we shared our canned food with them getting freshly baked bread against it. When we went back to our trenches to have a short rest for the fierce fights of next day. We were all thinking. What have we had anything to do in Gallipoli? O.K. We had fought in Sınai to secure Suez Canal. O.K. for the sake of Britain we went fighting in Middle East to save our Arab friends from cruel Turks. But who we were saving from whom in Gallipoli?

We all realized that we were not here to serve a patriotic purpose. We were here to save the prestige of British Admiralty minister who suggested to pass the navy through Dardanelles and failed.

Last week we were in a bayonet skirmish, chest to chest. Our friend Tom was near me, a shrapnel hit his head. It was unbearable to see a dying man when his limbs still move.

I recalled the days we played cricket with him. His mother aunt Vicky used to prepare food for us after each game. If I escape from hell and come back home, how can I say her that Tom died and I am alive? When I was looking at Tom with these thoughts I saw a Turkish soldier who was attacking me with his bayonet. I moved quicker and stabbed him in his stomach. His painful scream I still could not forget. If I had met him in normal time would I kill him?

Becky my love. Tomorrow army commanders will order us to kill. But no one in the world, after Gallipoli, will be able to order me, to hate. Hope to meet you again. Your John"

On May 7, Hasan was in the coffee house together with his father. The only entertainment means in those days was radio. Unfortunately few people had radios in their house. Coffee houses in the villages were ideal places in this respect where there were always radios. Villagers used to go coffee houses not only to meet their friends but to listen radio as well. By this way inexperienced young men had the chance to listen the interpretation of the old people. One announcement attracted the attention of everybody but mostly Hasan.

- According to the latest news; Lusitania cruise liner, set sail on May 6, from Liverpool was sunk by a German submarine today at London time

14.10 Latest information suggests that only 800 people out of 2000 could be saved. Among the casualties unfortunately most of them were women and children.

A sudden stroke paralyzed Hasan. He could not move neither talk for some time. His head fell on his arms. He started to cry loudly in screams. His father came near him. Pulled his head on his shoulder and asked what was up.

- My wife and my son were on the sinking Lusitania ship.

His father and coffee house attendees were speechless. They all loved Hasan but no one could say any word of consolation. Ali efendi pulled himself together quicker.

- Hasan my son. Is it not possible that your family will be among the rescued 800 people? Let's not hasten to grieve.
- No father I know they died. How can a little boy and a young woman stay alive out of that disaster? My most beloved reasons to live, are no more alive. All my future dreams were collapsed. My future darkened. I am already dead and I shall kill myself to make it true.

Hasan did not listen to any villagers until an idea came to his mind.

- Father, if you say not to grieve till everything is confirmed, then I request all of you not to tell anything to anybody about my decision, out of this coffee house today. People may talk between themselves, then mother can hear. We do not want to make her grieving before things are known firmly, do we? I made up a better decision now. I shall go to Gallipoli military office tomorrow and volunteer to fight in the frontier. If my family is alive I wish God save me. If they are dead however I will pray for martyrdom.
- Hasan, I know I cannot change your mind but think of your mother. If she learns the death of Jenny and Hakan, would it better to have you for saving her from a total collapse?
- Then tell her I started a new job in Istanbul. If our divine tragedy is to grieve we cannot change it, can we?

The battle started on May 18, lasted eight hours and Turks lost 3000 versus 160 of Anzacs. Towards the sun set, all were back in the trenches but none was on the field to help.

Whoever raised his head was being shot. John said,

- Kevin do you hear the screams of injured soldiers? They are calling for help.
- Of course I do. But if we help them we shall be shot.

- Kevin we could be in their place. We should do something.

    An Anzac soldier came close to the trench and fell in.

- Oh my God!!! This soldier has no right leg. He has severe bleeding. If Simpson does not come, he will die. In two minutes Simpson from Red Cross service, appeared with his donkey. They loaded the injured soldier on saddle and rushed to the shore where emergency service was operating. Before the sun rise there were few screams coming from the battle field. Suddenly a thunderous shout came from the Turkish side "ALLAH ALLAH". Turks were attacking. Three of them jumped in John's trench. John was awake and ready with his gun. He shot the first one. But the other soldier speared Kevin at his sleep. John easily shot the second one as well before Bill came to help. He could defend himself against the third and the last one if his foot had not hit the dead body of Kevin. While falling Bill had given the chance to his opponent shoot him at heart. John killed the last soldier as well but could not be happy since in 20 seconds he had lost his 20 years old, two friends. The Turkish attacks, to draw back Anzacs from their standings, lasted 18 hours. Anzacs could not be driven away, both sides were exhausted.

The worse than this, unattended corpses were spreading a badly smell when decaying.

A staff lieutenant came into the trench. Friends if we continue to fight with these decaying bodies, we shall die by sickness rather than the bullets. We want to come to a cease fire agreement with Turks. We are looking for a volunteer to take a white flag in one hand to show our peaceful intention and an Australian flag to other showing our identity and confirming to have no gun in our hand. Can any of you wish to do this?

- I can do it sir.
- Thank you John. Here, white and Australian flags.

John got out of the trench doing exactly what he was ordered and shouting in English.

"I am from peace envoy. I want to talk to you"

Turkish commanders ordered the soldiers to stop firing. One of them could not hear the lieutenant voice. He targeted John and fired. John received a large wound on his arm and fell down. Turkish and Anzac soldiers were frozen. Right at that moment Hasan moved forward. He ran near Anzac soldier. He took the white flag from him, wrapped the wound and tightly tied above the wound. Hasan took the Australian flag from ground and then lifted John in his arms. He walked to the Australian trench. He gently carried John into the trench, left him on a soft soldier dress. He handed the flag over lieutenant. He apologized for the mistake with a perfect Oxford accent and confirmed the acceptance of ceasefire agreement. Lieutenant Steve was perplexed. A Turkish soldier had not only saved the life of an Anzac but lifted the Australian flag from ground and handed it over him respectfully. But he was more amazed with the gesture of Turkish soldier who came near John and talked friendly.

- How are you my friend? I wish you quick recovery. My name is Hasan. I apologize for the mistake my friends did.

    John was feeling better and he knew it was because of this Turkish soldier who tied his wound and stopped bleeding.

- My name is John and I am really obliged to you Hasan. Please give me your address and take my military identity from my pocket. If we survive over this nonsense fight I want to write you and be your loyal friend. I want to declare the whole world who was Anzacs best friend and my savior in the battle of Gallipoli. Hasan told his address to Steve to take note and left the trench.

    In the meantime soldiers had left their trenches. With Hasan translation, commanders decided where to bury the corpses. The graveyard holes were dug out jointly. Soldiers helped each other to carry the corpses and cover them with soil. After 18 hours of fierce fight, they had to work hard another two hours to pay the last respect to their fallen. Strong wind had wiped away the smell of the corpses. But what could wipe away the sin of humanity in Gallipoli? On departure, commanders wished good luck to each other in tearful eyes. They would fight tomorrow may be killing each other to honor their country but they would be bound eternally when generations remember Gallipoli battle.

2 weeks later it happened again. Turks planned a decisive attack on Anzacs. They were capturing the Anzac trenches one by one. Only a machine gun still firing on a hill was delaying them. Turkish commander asked someone to volunteer stopping that Anzac gun.

- With your permission I will stop that gun.
- O.K. Hasan god save you.

Hasan filled his rifle with bullets in one hand. He took a grenade to his other hand and started to run in zig zags. He threw the hand grenade on to the shield. He had stopped the gun but could not clean the shield. He jumped into the trench and was shot from his back. Lieutenant Steve immediately recognized who was shot while falling.

- Hasan, what damned did I do, unknowingly?

Hasan too had recognized the lieutenant

- Don't be sorry Steve. By killing me you do a great favor. My wife and son died in a sea accident after which I did not want to live. I intentionally volunteered most dangerous tasks in military. I am happy now to meet them soon.

Hasan could not speak more and died in the arms of Steve Who was crying loudly and complaining.

- Oh Gallipoli. How cruel you were that you forced us to kill our friends. How elevated you were on the other hand that you taught us to love our enemies. We are losing the battle of Gallipoli. But we are winning the essence of Anzac spirit which will comprise of courage, courtesy and caring.

Next day Ali efendi received a telegraph from New York and informed Fatma laughingly.

- Fatma good news. Jenny and Hakan arrived New York.
- Have they gone to New York Ali? You did not tell me.
- Don't ask me Fatma. The ship Lusitania they got on board at Liverpool was sunk by a German

submarine. Before getting a confirmation I did not know the truth either.

Thank god that among the 800 rescued ones, out of 2000 there were Hakan and Jenny. My nightmares ended.

- Ali efendi. I do not know whether I should be happy or sad? It is good news that they were safely arrived New York. But bad news to know that they will live in the USA.
- Take it from good side Fatma. If we had lost them in the accident, would it be better than their living in New York?

Besides we do not know what future holds for Turkey and Europe. But a life in USA is safer forever.

But the nightmares of Ali efendi proved to be real. Ten days later than this conversation, bad news came in. Hasan had fallen martyr at Gallipoli. All villagers in his funeral was crying. Fatma hatun was fainted and could not manage to stand up. She complained God plenty.

- O my Lord. If you would take him so early why did you destine his birth? Why did you not let a young man, who is both Robert College and Oxford graduate, serve his country? Why you destine our country to be humiliated by the loss of precious young generation. Why an obedient woman like me, should continuously had bad fate.

15

POST 1915 EVENTS

In March 1917 a revolution in Russia overthrown the last tsar. What impact could it have on Turkey? German and Turkish staff members were in debate.

- This revolution came just in time after the Dardanelles and Gallipoli victories. We can now move our forces from Caucasus to Egypt to encounter Britain. We can regain the Sınai Peninsula. We should also give a lesson to the Emir of Hejaz who made an agreement with agent Lawrence.

German general, Falkenhein listens in amazement.

- Gentlemen I have difficulty understanding. You evaluate a world war as a matter of your own revenge. When Britain was firmly settled in Egypt over the years you speak about settlement and giving lesson to Emir of Hejaz.

- I have difficulty to understand you general. Will Ottoman Empire not clean the stains in the history?
- While you attempt to clean the stains, what if you make the new ones? In Gallipoli Turkish army was weakened and had no trust in anybody but Mustafa Kemal. Who will command your troops in Egypt?
- We do not trust Mustafa Kemal either. You know he suggests to concentrate our forces on Syria, Palestine. Bagdad line and forget the rest.
- I heard many praising words about Mustafa Kemal from general Liman Von Sanders but I had not thought he could be that much the master of strategy.
- General you will almost say he is superior to us.
- I do not know if you are superior to him but I sign all his words. The people in Mesopotamian area are still your friends. At least not your enemies as they are in Egypt. If you stabilize oil rich territories than you take revenge from Britain. You neglected west Thrace while there were still people of your ethnicity and you lost. You almost distribute your territories free of charge where you can send ammunition much easier.
- General. Do you forget Hejaz-Istanbul railway.
- No I don't. It is the first target to be thought for a sabotage.

What will you do if the railway is bombed while carrying the army. You will then stay in the middle of a desert.

- General Falkenhein you may have good reasons but Egypt is very important for us.
- Don't be misled by illusions. You lost Egypt 100 years ago.

I mean for Egyptians you are not important. Khedives made secret agreements with Britain long time ago

- Did our religious brothers do this betrayal?
- Yes they did. We captured a letter which reads as follows.
- Dear mother. I so much hate Turks that I easily came to agreement with British agents.
- That is why we want to give them their lessons.
- Gentlemen instead of giving lessons why don't you try to take lessons. You try to command a fight, thousand miles away, from your desk in Istanbul. You will surely destroy yourself but your greatest harm will be to the Empire.

In the meantime British cabinet is in the meeting.

It is difficult to understand gentlemen. We attacked two times but could not capture Gazza. Moreover the people of Gazza is on our side.

- Prime Minister, there are three reasons why we failed. First we underestimated the Turks, like in Gallipoli. Second Istanbul-Hejaz railway system is still operative. Last but not the least British general in charge of the operation commands the battle from Savoy hotel in Cairo.
- What do you suggest then?
- First we replace the general in command. I recommend General Allenby. Then we tell Emir of Hejaz that he should either destroy the railway or forget Palestine. Lastly we provoke a revolt in Bagdad to divide the Turkish forces.

The plan was put into implementation successfully. Railway was sabotaged first. But at that time Turks had already arrived Gazza. They were planning a surprise attack on British forces. The chance of this plan was quite big. But Palestinians informed this plan to General Allenby. When Turkish army attacked, British forces were waiting to trap. Most of the Turkish soldiers lost their lives after this treason. Allenby continued to march and captured not only Gazza but Jerusalem as well. When Allenby entered Gazza the Palestinians were crazily applauding him.

The moral collapse of this defeat was great on Turks. Soon after this, they lost both Bagdad and west Thrace. When allied forces won the war, Ottoman Empire took part on the losing side. Union & Progress party leaders are in meeting.

- Friends we lost on all frontiers by giving up an area of 10 million square kilometers. Ottoman Empire declined.
- I think best to do is to accept British mandate and to save remaining territories with their support.
- If we would accept British mandate why had we not come to agreement with them before? Some of us had predicted.
- What did we do against these clever words? Made a secret agreement with Germans. We stubbornly fought with Britain in the Middle East and Egypt.
- I learned Mustafa Kemal was sent to Anatolia by sultan to bring, fall apart armies together and stop the revolt. I wrote him a letter to contact British officers.
- My poor friends. Do we think we still run the country? If we have slightest honor should we not resign?
- Of course we shall resign. But is it not good if Mustafa Kemal benefits from our experiences?
- What experience pasha. If he is slightly clever he does just the opposite of our recommendations and does not sink the country as we did.

16

A STRATEGY GENIUS TAKES THE COMMAND

With an agreement between Britain and Ottoman Empire made on October 30, 1918. Turks had to leave their arms. Mustafa Kemal geniously checks, all the moves of allied nations, after the truce, like a player in the chess game.

November 13, 1918: Mustafa Kemal sees the navy of allied forces in Istanbul on return to the city.

April 30, 1919: Mustafa Kemal is assigned by sultan Vahidettin, as the inspector of the 9 th army in Anatolia.

May, 15, 1919: Greek army occupies Izmir in west Anatolia by the approval of allied nations.

May 19 – June 21, 1919: Mustafa Kemal first sets foot in Samsun in North West Anatolia. He issues Amasya declaration about the unity of Turkey.

June 23, 1919: Istanbul government disapproves this declaration and calls him back.

September 4-13, 1919: Sivas congress meet and declare the independence of the country.

March 16, 1920: Allied forces occupies Istanbul, dissolves the last parliament of the Ottoman Empire.

April 23, 1920: Mustafa Kemal opens the first Grand National Assembly in Ankara.

June 10, 1920: Istanbul government signs the Sevres treaty disintegrating Anatolia by distributing among the allied nations and Greece.

June 22, 1920: Greeks occupy Bursa, in western Anatolia. January 6-10, 1921: Greek army is stopped by Inonu battle

March 23 – April 1, 1921: Greeks are defeated in the second Inonu battle.

July 10, 1921: Greek army occupies Eskisehir. August 5, 1921: Mustafa Kemal is assigned Commander in chief with absolute authority by National Grand Assembly.

August 23, – September 13, 1921: Greek army marching on Ankara is defeated in Sakarya.

These achievements, made the members of Grand National Assembly quite hasty and get into conflict with Mustafa Kemal.

Urgency said: Bursa was occupied we should regain it.

Prudency objected: We can't wear out our army so early.

Old Ottoman mentality thought: If we do not get back occupied territory enemy will further advance.

Battlefield genius knew: The more enemy spreads in a vast territory the less powerful they will remain.

Out-fashioned conservatives asked: To set line of defense.

Revolutionary mind: Introduced a new concept to the war history. There is no line defense but surface defending.

When Greeks had no hope to advance Ankara, they decided to keep what they had earned in Anatolia. They set up the strongest defense line between Eskisehir - Afyon line. They dug out trenches in months, erecting iron fences in front of them. They fortified the line with machine guns.

Military experts predicted that this line could not be broken in less than 6 months. At last the commander, predicting beyond the horizons, gave his last command on August 26, 1922. "Armies your first target is Mediterranean. March on"

Turkish army broke all defense lines, won the decisive victory on August 30, 1922. Turkish army Recaptured Izmir on September 9 and Istanbul on October 6.

British Prime Minister Lloyd George defined the outcome with the following words.

"Our plan, to disintegrate Ottoman Empire and distribute Anatolia among us, was perfect. But look at our misfortune that a genius, would come only once in hundred years, was born at our time."

But he was not the only one, impressed from Mustafa Kemal. Venizelos, the prime Minister of Greece, offered Kemal as the candidate to Nobel peace prize, for initiating the Balkan pact for peace and friendship after the war.

17

GALLIPOLI VISITORS

The decisive victory, which made Turks greatly happy, had some natural consequences:

January 19, 1922: Lloyd George cabinet resigned as once Winston Churchill did after Gallipoli.

November 1, 1922: Sultanate was abrogated. November 17, 1922: The last sultan Vahidettin left the country in a British ship.

July 24, 1923: Lausanne treaty was signed between Turkey and allied forces; crowning the victory of Turks and sealing the independence of Turkish Republic.

October 29, 1923: Turkish Republic was founded.

The happiness of Ali aga in Gallipoli was two folded. Their son Husein was graduated from primary school. Had it been the country under occupation it would be a problem to decide which school Husein would continue. But now situation was different. Ali aga enrolled his son to Robert College in Istanbul as a boarding student.

A letter came from Australia revived their sorrow.

"Hasan. I write this letter to you without knowing if you could survive Gallipoli? I hope you are still alive like me.

Long years passed over Gallipoli. But I have not forgotten you and Gallipoli even one moment. I told everybody how you saved my life carrying me out of the battlefield. After you brought me to the trench, Simpson took me to one of Anzac ships on his donkey. When I arrived Sydney, I found my sweetheart Becky got married to my best friend Zach. As my father passed away, mom met me with great happiness. My brother Frank was at school age he could not help mom. I had to work hard to put our farm into order. But Gallipoli remained my incurable obsession. In order to forget you and other Anzacs who had fallen on the battlefield, I worked like hell on our farm. I first repaired the folds of the animals. I added cold storage to our slaughter house. I increased the production capacity of our dairy. I visited the retailers in Australia to sell our products. This hard work was physically tiring but mentally relaxing for me. I don't need of worrying about my family now. Frank can take over the responsibility of the farm from me. So I can plan to visit Gallipoli to recall the burning but loving memories. By the way what I read on papers about Turkey, excited me. I was very proud in learning that the Lausanne treaty was signed and Turkey became an independent republic. I was delighted that the legendary Mustafa Kemal had been elected as the first president of Turkey. Then I found your address note which I kept on the upper pocket of my uniform for years. If you live, I want to visit all the places where Anzacs and Turks not only wrote a legend of heroism but humanity as well. I hope you are still alive and we realize our dreams to establish firm friendship between Australia and Turkey. John White"

Ali aga and Fatma had not only recalled but learned a phase of the life of their son. He had not only fought but also saved the life of the enemy, on the battlefield.

Ali aga answered the letter immediately.

"My dear John. Unfortunately I lost Hasan. But fortunately you are alive. I lost one son. But I won thousands sons as the brave soldiers who fought in Gallipoli. Your letter pleased me greatly. Please do not change your plan, you intended to do, if Hasan had lived. Come to Turkey. Let us visit Gallipoli together. You tell us the real story of Gallipoli battle, unfortunately we could not learn from Hasan. I shall show you the historical Istanbul. The only city standing on two continents and the capital of three empires. A whole Turkish villagers are waiting you to realize your dreams for establishing a firm friendship between Anzacs and Turks.

I hope you come. Ali. The father of all Gallipoli veterans."

Two weeks later Ali received another letter from New York.

"Dear father. It has been almost ten years that we are far away from each other. But I continuously follow Turkey.

It was pleasing to know that Hasan died, on a precious cause and Turkey won the Battle of Independence. Lausanne treaty and the proclamation of the Turkish Republic were further achievements proving the continuation of Gallipoli spirit. Hakan knows his father died in Gallipoli. But he still asks a lot about Hasan. Neither Hakan nor I, could forget him. He wants to know his grandfather and grandmother. Next year in May, he will graduate from Primary school. I want to promise him a visit to Turkey as a graduation gift, if it is convenient for you. From Jenny and Hakan with love."

This letter made Ali aga and his family very happy. Fatma was praying every day. She was suspicious to see her grandson after the martyrdom of Hasan. Now it would come true. She would see both Hakan and Jenny. Ali aga wrote Jenny signing together with Fatma and informed to be waiting them enthusiastically.

In March 1924, Ali aga received a letter from Australia.

"Dear father of my friend Hasan. As much as I was sorry to learn Hasan's death so much I have been happy with your invitation. I come to Istanbul in mid-April. Even if I will not see Hasan, to remember him on the battlefield, has been an obsession for me. I am anxious to meet you soon.

Respectfully yours. John White"

Ali aga wrote John to meet Husein in Robert College. By this way he would have chance to see Istanbul and Husein would take him to Gallipoli very easily. It was very sensitive for both Hasan's parents and John to meet each other. They requested John over and over to tell how Hasan carried him on the battlefield and saved his life. Husein was also proud with the heroic stories of his brother.

Ali aga decided to show John the surrounding before taking him to Gallipoli. John was both intellectual and sensitive. He used to walk on rocky and sandy beaches long hours. He liked to watch the sailing of the fishing boats before sun rises and waiting for their return at sun set times. He was a very good swimmer like all Australians and scuba diver to spear one day a five kilogram sea bass. He visited the folds and dairy with Ali aga and recommended him new way of cream cheese production.

Ali aga appreciated John by everyday he knew him. On a hot spring morning they rode on their horses to visit sacred places where thousands lost their lives. On their way to battlefield, they gave breaks for lunch and rests. It was about the sun set time. Although they were very close to destination, they were tired to continue. Ali aga entered a coffee house. After learning the name of esteemed aga of the village he walked to his table and greeted.

- Good evening Husmen aga. I am Ali aga from Yayla village. I wanted to take my Australian guest to the battlefield who once fought there. But it is late now to continue. Can you find us a place to stay at night?
- What does it mean Ali aga, if I can find a place for you? Both of you, are my guests tonight. After having your coffees we shall go my home for dinner. Ali aga translated the conversation to John. They followed Husmen aga to his house. When they arrived home, they saw the wife of Husmen aga was grilling some meats in the garden and two daughters were preparing the table. When they went to bed room they saw two beds. John asked.
- Ali aga how come the guest room is so big? Linens look new and pillows are so clean?
- John, the room is big because this is Husmen aga's own bedroom. They probably use the

linens first time for us. It is not custom here to offer guests unclean staff.

When they woke up, one of the daughters brought them towels as to be used after washing the hands. Husmen aga was waiting them in front of a magnificent breakfast table. He asked their health. John thanked Husmen aga and his family for their hospitality. He then explained how did he meet Hasan and why did he come to Gallipoli again. Tear drops filled Husmen aga's eyes. His cousin too had fallen victim in the battle. Before leaving he suggested.

- Ali aga. I put your horses into my fold. If you permit me, I would like to take you to the cemetery with my coach and visit my cousin. Let your horses stay here, you take them on your return. John tried to object not to disturb Husmen aga. But he has been stopped by Ali aga.
- What do you do John? It is great impoliteness in this area to refuse an aga.
- What a courteous man is he? To open his house and give his bed to us.
- John, if you set on road in Thrace and the whole Anatolia you do not need to worry about where to stay. If you knock the door of any house on your way, you will be given bed as to be a guest of God. I did not knock any door because I have

to ask it definitely from aga of the district. An aga cannot ignore another aga.

On the battlefield, John exactly spotted where Hasan carried himself. This was the most sensitive moment for all.

- Husmen aga, I would never think to find such hospitality. I have been bewitched by the manners here. I met a lot of Gallipoli veterans in Australia but I have not seen any single one who was not loving their fiercest opponents. You know we celebrate Anzac day every year on April 25, where only the countries have not been in war with us, join the parade. Turkey is the only exception to take part in the parade. I am very pleased to come here and meet you.
- If you had loved us that much John you can stay here as long as you wish. You have experience in sheep breeding and dairy business and I need someone who can help me in farming. Our cooperation will be a perfect match.
- Thank you Ali aga. I shall start working for you at the closest time. Coming to how long I would stay, let us have a test period and get know each other. We decide at end of autumn. It was early May. Ali aga decided to take John to Hıdırellez fests. He took Zeynep with him and went Salim aga's village. John watched the show in pleasure. He jumped on fire and drew a wish. When they

read it, he was amazed. "You come from far away, you have love pain in your heart, and you will find in shortest day, a lady to love again." He was really suffering love pain since Becky left him. He did not have a serious relationship with anybody after that.

When they returned home they found a letter sent by Jenny from New York.

"Dear father. I made our reservation to-day with Hakan.

Our Paris-Istanbul train will arrive Sirkeci station on June 15, at 12 o'clock noon time. Hakan and I, are very excited for meeting you soon. Jenny and Hakan"

This letter brought great joy and curiosity to Ali aga family. Fatma was the most anxious one. She had not so far seen any of them. Hakan should have been a big boy. She had always prayed to see him and God granted her prayers when she had lost her hopes.

At last the day had come. Ali aga and Husein went Istanbul One day earlier and checked in Pera palas hotel where they would altogether stay few days to show the visitors some of Istanbul sight-seeing. They heard the announcement of coming Paris train. Ali aga was waiting them in front row but sleeping wagons were in the rear. Still he saw the young boy very much resembling Hasan near a blond woman. Jenny also had noticed her father-in-law. They ran each other to be embraced longingly. Ali aga had liked his grandson and daughter-in-law at first sight. Hakan had found his uncle Husein friendly, at his age speaking good English. Ali aga first took them to Konyali meat restaurant. The first time Jenny and Hakan was tasting Turkish specialties like doner and shish kebabs. Such delicious meats they had tried neither in London nor in New York. Sweets, like baklava and chicken breast were tasty too.

Visitors stayed three more days in Istanbul to see more of the city. Jenny had never seen in London or New York, 1500 years old Cathedrals like Hagia Sophia and Hagia Ireni or older monuments like obelisk, underground cistern and city walls. In Topkapi palace they appreciated the magnificence of Ottoman Empire. In archaeology museum they admired the marble sarcophagus of Alexander the great, stone lion reliefs from the hanging gardens of Babylon and first written treaty in history between Rameses and Hittite king, in hieroglyph on a stone tablet, 3300 years ago. Jenny shopped in Grand Bazaar where close to 4000 shops under one roof were still operative. They made a Bosphorus cruise disembarking at Bebek to show the College where Husein was attending. Not only Hakan but also Jenny amazed. It was difficult to find such a location in the world. They learned that it was the first American college abroad. Next day they watched golden horn from

Galata tower, enjoyed Marmara Sea from Princes Island and looked at Istanbul from Chamlica hill. It was now the time to head to the final destination. When arrived at Gallipoli it was late in the evening but everybody was waiting them. Next day Husein took Hakan to fishing.

They returned close to noon time not only with fish but shrimps and mussels as well. Fatma was happy to offer fresh sea food to her dearest guests. Afternoon was the time to pay respect to deceased family members. Ali aga took them to the village cemetery. After visiting the few others they came to Hasan's grave. Hakan stood silent near father. But Jenny could not control herself. She cried, sobbing loudly. Ali aga could hardly stopped his daughter-in-law, pressing her head over his chest. Jenny, before leaving, kissed the soil and tomb stone of her husband several times.

At dinner table there was one more plate for someone else whom Jenny had not met. After starting work near Ali aga, John used to come dinner to give daily reports to his boss.

Ali aga had given him the old annex in the garden which used to be lodged by the servants. So Jenny and Hakan met John at dinner table. They did not talk too much at the table. After dinner Jenny listened the story of John.

-If I am here today Jenny and able to talk to you that is because of Hasan. I came out the trench with a white flag to announce cease fire. Turkish commander ordered to stop firing. But one soldier did not hear and shot me at arm which was bleeding like streams. Hasan shouted in such a loud voice that everybody left the guns. He ran near me. I felt an iron claw pressed my arm. He tightly tied the bruise with white flag. He took me in his arm like a child and gently brought to the trench. I have therefore been very much pleased to meet his wife and son to night.

Jenny recalled her first night with Hasan. He had taken her with wedding dress like a child and carried to the bed. Every moment from that night on, she had lived in heaven.

- He was strong but gentle John.
- Do I not know Jenny? When he left me on a dress in the trench, I realized an Australian flag in his hand. He had not only lifted me but also had picked up my falling flag, to hand over to our lieutenant respectfully.
- Jenny recalled her rescue from Lusitania, arriving New York safely with her son and receiving the letter which ended all her happiness. It was 9 years passed over this tragedy she was still alone in life. She could hardly sleep in the night.

In the morning she found her son near her bed who reminded her breakfast time and visit to Yayla village.

Jenny wanted to see the battlefield where her husband had lost his life. Hakan too was willing to go to the place. Ali aga had something to do in Istanbul. John suggested.

- Ali aga if you permit I can take them to the battlefield with Husein. In the morning the coach was taking them to the place, through the Dardanelles strait. John stopped the coach at some point.
- Jenny, Hakan look at this spot. It is called narrow. Turks first stopped the allied navy here. Some ships were sunk by mines and some by the battery fire of Turks. They had to retreat and tried to find another way through Gallipoli. British admiralty minister was so much irritated with his failing attempt that he suggested Gallipoli landing.
- Do you mean that in order to save their prestige, they drove so many young people to death?
- That is unfortunately true Jenny. As a matter of fact, both he and the prime minister had to resign after Gallipoli.
- Damned them all. Can resignation bring back so many young men? That is a hidden criminal act, unpunished.
- You are absolutely right Jenny. They ordered fake stories to historians, by declaring the soldiers as patriotic heroes they escaped from punishment.

- Did they really John? Lord cannot be so unjust. They must at least have been punished in after world life.
- After witnessing all the pains in the battle, I say Amen.

After passing the strait they saw a vegetable field with red and big tomatoes in it. They had their lunch packs in the coach but not tomatoes. Husein asked the farmer.

- Can you give some tomatoes to us?
- Take this basket, get in the field and collect as much as you wish. They walked in the field. First time in their life they smelled the fresh tomato flavor spreads around, when they are broken from their stalk. It was not like a perfume but very much appetizing. Tomato was red but the spot on hand was green. Jenny took a bite. It was so delicious that she could not stop herself eating the whole. The others who followed Jenny by taking a bite, did the same.
- Jenny asked their debt to the farmer through Husein
- What debt brother? I saw there are foreigners among you.

They are our guests. Jenny tried to object when Husein translated. John stopped her.

- What do you do Jenny? Refusing what you are offered is an impoliteness that cannot be tolerated.

Jenny was amazed first. But then she recalled Hasan. He was too, so generous as to be called gentleman among friends. They first went to the landing beach. They would both listen John's war memories and have their lunch.

Driver Selim usta, prepared services on the rug. He put meat balls, stuffed vegetables and pastry on plates. Glasses and water jugs were also placed with freshly baked bread. When they started the lunch they ate them with tomato to make tastier. After the lunch John told them the first day of landing. Where did the fleet cast anchor. Where soldiers stepped on soil? From which point the machine gun fire came on them with which, most of the first runners fell down. The weather was nice. Hakan and Husein were sweating. They wished to swim in the mirror-like water. Jenny wished to see the trenches. Selim usta stayed with young boys on the beach. Jenny and John continued to climb the hill. Hakan and Husein would join them after the swimming.

John, held Jenny's hand to help her. Jenny asked.

- The hill is too steep. Had it not been difficult to climb?
- It was difficult Jen. On top of it, we had to carry a heavy rifle and bag. That is why the greatest casualty we had on the first day while climbing hill, Turks hunted most of us.
- We came here passing another flat beach with no hill. Would it not be easier to land from that point John?
- We would have certainly less casualty Jen. But admiral in charge of this operation, anchored here in the darkness of the night. Then he wished to hide his mistake from the admiralty. He has not changed his command on account of the thousands lives.
- Has my son left orphan because of that? Have I been enslaved to loneliness to save the prestige of a few men?

They had come to a muddy and sliding end on the slope. John told Jenny firmly grab a small tree on the slope. He first pulled up himself. Then pulled Jenny with his one hand. She unwillingly thought about who could be stronger? John, who pulled up herself or Hasan, who carried John on the battle field? She asked John to get rid of her thoughts

- How a soldier can climb this hill John, with rifle?

- If he cannot, he is shot Jenny. The problem is; the man on the ship, does not mind this and his name is engraved on man of honor plate in the war museum.

John took Jenny to the place where Hasan carried him. The distance between the trenches in some points were less than 30 feet. How courageous these soldiers were, that they fought there? What kind of a heart her husband had, that he left his trench to save the life of an enemy? The man who was so brave, had been her husband for many happy days. In civil life he was afraid of harming an ant.

He was afraid of discontent his wife and son for any wish of them. She could not stand longer and started to cry. John gently held her to console. She continued to cry on his chest, while feeling the stiffness of John's muscles. They could not stand longer before their lips touched on each other. They almost pushed each other when heard the voices of the boys.

On return way they were tired to talk too much. The boys were asleep. Jenny was thinking. Her husband had lost his life in rudity where no place was lack of beauty, no man had any feeling of animosity. How could a man carry an enemy risking his own life? She had gradually understood it. Trojans had fought Greeks but loved them to keep their wooden horse as a memory from the enemy. They had killed each other on the field but mourned after the fight. Greek mythology writer, Homeros by telling the story of Troy had described Gallipoli as well. Jenny thought of herself. She had never been so sensitive after losing Hasan. She looked at her son. Having Hakan near her, she could not think of any other love so far. She had always a resistance against others to protect the love of Hasan in her heart. But now everybody was attracting her. She had loved her parents-in-law, her brother-in-law, driver Selim, dairy tender Recai, fishermen on the shore, tomato farmer on the way. She then looked at John. He had come from Far East and his way intersected with hers from far west. They were here to pay tribute to the same man, whose memories had pushed everybody away from Jenny till today. But John had been the exception now. Was it a divine destiny or the last wish of a caring husband?

Next day Jenny and her parents were sitting around the tea table. Hakan, Husein and John watering the flowers in the garden. Husein asked John.

- John, can you take me and Hakan to sardine fishing?
- Ask your parents boys. If they permit, I will love to do.

In the morning after breakfast they were back from hunt.

Jenny watched her son. Husein was carrying the basket full of fish. Hakan was following John. He told the story.

Mom, John taught me how to lay down the nets. We pulled up the nets together before sun rise and collected fish with Husein. Look at the basket how much we caught. At noon time boys helped John to grill the sardines by wrapping in grape leaves. Freshly caught sardines were delicious. At afternoon sleep Hakan was talking Jenny.

Mom, thank you for taking me here. Every day I learn something new. The people are very nice. I love my grandparents. I am very friendly with Husein and John. They behave me nicely.

- I loved these Gallipoli people too. They have dignity and love in their hearts
- What do you think about John? He is as good as Turks.
- You are right. He is always smiling and ready to help.
- He is also very strong. Was my father strong too?
- He was a strong and loving man. Think he went war because he thought we died in the accident.
- I am very proud of him, mom. I am proud of all soldiers who fought in Gallipoli, including John. They have not lost their loves, even at killing and dying.

- You are right Hakan. They have not lost their loves but their beloved ones, lost them.

It was mid-August. Jenny and Hakan were departing two weeks later. On a day Hakan and Husein planned to go fishing and Ali aga had business meeting in Istanbul, John took Jenny to sunflower and rice farms. Half meter long sun flowers, were fully covering the fields. Moving under the wind they were stretching down to the sea where blue and yellow colors were blending magnificently. John and Jenny entered into the sunflowers. They ate the sweet seeds sharing their food with bees. They rode on horses to see the rice fields. On either sides of a stream there were plantations on which many young barefoot girls were harvesting the crop, with a basket in their arms.

Jenny had a short pants on her. She could not wait longer put of her shoes and stepped on mud. They gave her a basket in which she put rice stalks. She was amusing and singing as she walked in the mud. Wet soil had taken away her fatigue from legs. Half an hour later she rode on her horse with her bare feet to go to the stream.

She washed her face, feet and hands. She saw John.

He was constantly looking her without talking.

- You do not talk John. Won't you say something?

- Yes I will Jen. Will you marry me?

    Jenny had liked John but she was not expecting such a question. She answered some time later.

- Don't you think we are the people of different worlds?
- You and Hasan also were the people of different worlds. Were you not? But you had the happiest marriage. We came here from the different parts of the world. You came here as an American and I was an Australian. As Anatolia had been the melting pot of more than 30 civilizations, this land blended us. We have both been Anatolian here.
- You are right John but I was so sorry after losing my husband I have not thought any relationship.
- When I left Gallipoli and went to Sydney I was equally sorry, to find my fiancée, married to my best friend. I have not so far thought, as you, to marry someone else. But that was not because I was happy to be alone. It was because I have not found anybody whom I could love. When I met you here, I knew I found the one whom I was looking for.

    I knew that happiness was dependent on coincidences which was not repeatable. If Hasan had not saved my life or if he knew your safe arrival to New York, he would not volunteered for Gallipoli, we would not meet. Would we? Intersecting our ways in Gallipoli is a divine destiny. But if we do not understand our fate we might not have a second chance. Are you ready to a lifelong loneliness Jen?

- Of course not John. But when I said we were from different parts of the world I meant our home. If we marry where we shall live for instance?
- Of course in USA Jen. You have your responsibilities connecting you to USA. But I have not such a strong tie with Australia. I left the responsibility of our farm to my brother already. In this case my homeland will be where my sweetheart is. I am a college graduate. If you wish I can start law education or take any other job. My target in life is to make you happy and be a good friend to your son. They got married in a church and returned to USA as a happy married couple.

Fatma had released all her troubles. It was the proper time now to realize her dreams and visit Mecca for pilgrimage. The nice part of this plan was, her in-laws Salim aga and his wife Kadriye hatun had also reserved their seats for the same. Fatma would not be lonely in a foreign country.

One day Ali aga ordered his driver to prepare his coach to go to dairy. Driver Selim took his son Mehmet with them. They went to dairy. Selim usta asked his son to untie the horses and take them to the fold. Young boy and horses encountered two big dogs on the way to the fold. Horses scared from the dogs and reared their heads. Mehmet had fallen down. One of the horses fell on Mehmet's leg. Mehmet screamed so loudly with the pain that his father and Ali aga ran to him. Poor boy had fainted from pain. One of his legs was badly broken. They put him on a stretcher.

They took him to Gallipoli military hospital. Doctors could stop his pain but unable to cure the broken leg. After two weeks, doctors reported their regrets that Mehmet was doomed to crutches. When Husein came home, he learned the accident. Mehmet was his childhood friend and should not have lived as disable for the rest of his life. He wrote a letter to Jenny with doctor report. Letter came from Jenny.

"Dear Husein. I checked with the doctors here the situation of Mehmet. They said, broken bones can be fixed to metal plaque here and removed after six months, when Mehmet would completely recover and walk without any problem. I talked John. We shall cover all operation expenses here and host him at our house if you can send him to USA."

They read the letter to driver Selim usta who started to cry and kissed the hands of Ali aga and Fatma hatun. Husein checked the cost of a return trip to USA via France by train and New York by ocean cruiser. It was $ 4000 which was impossible to afford by Ali aga himself under the difficult conditions of the country. Fatma learned the situation from Ali aga. She was deeply sorry to know that a young boy would stay disable for the rest of his life. She recalled drivers crying and kissing their hands when learned his son could be cured. At breakfast table she talked to Ali aga.

- Ali aga I thought all night long and decided to send Mehmet for recovery with the money I saved for pilgrimage.
- Are you giving up the pilgrimage you planned for years?
- I cannot go anywhere, knowing that a young boy will stay disable for the rest of his life.

Everybody was crying around the table. Young wife of Ali aga stood up from the table, kissed the hands of Fatma. Six months later Mehmet returned Gallipoli walking with no aid.

18

THE YOUNGHOOD
DAYS OF HUSEIN

In June 1932 Husein, graduated from Istanbul Robert College. The parents and grandparents were ready and proud in the ceremony. Salim aga and Kadriye hatun have never been regretted to approve their daughter Zeynep's marriage with Ali aga. The result was a brilliant grandson today. Husein came to Gallipoli to have a rest in summer and make a decision for his higher education. They received a pleasing letter from New York. John, Jenny and Hakan congratulated Husein for graduation and invited him, if he wants to continue in USA. His father Ali aga was still under the influence of sultan Hamid. He was of the opinion that after the acceptance of Latin alphabet, one language would not be enough for young generations. He had desires to provide his son the best opportunities to find the best job in a multinational. He wished his son to continue his career in a better post war environment.

Besides, USA had not yet overcome 1929 financial crisis.

He wrote a letter to Helga.

"Dear Helga and Hans Peter. My son Husein finished Robert College this year. Of course he speaks perfect English. But I want him to learn German as well. I also wish him to continue my career attending a university to learn civil engineering. I shall appreciate if you could help him."

Two weeks later he received the answer from Germany.

"Ali. We have been very pleased with Husein's graduation.

Would we not help your son to be an engineer, if his father had been the architect of our happiness? We shall host him at home. Our daughter Gabriella went yesterday to the university from where you were graduated. They recalled you and made provisional registration of your son. You just inform us when he will be in Berlin. The rest we'll take care. Helga and Hans Peter.

This letter had pleased Ali aga and excited Husein. A new page in his life was opening. He was lucky to have the friends of his father in Berlin.

Husein was met in station by Helga and Hans Peter. They behaved him very friendly. Their house was quite big and comfortable. The bedroom given to Husein was large. Just before the dinner their only child Gabriella came in. Husein had attended

German courses in College. He had no difficulty in communicating with them.

Gabi, was rather a mature woman. She had her mother's beauty but not with the same softness. She had not married and was one of the chiefs of the youth camps. Young German generation used to attend these camps on vacations to be raised as ideal youth for the future. She explained their targets after dinner.

- Husein you know Germany and the Ottoman Empire were allies in World War I. We have never forgotten our friendship. We always loved Turks. Your father has been the best friend of my parents. Unfortunately Germany could not have a leader like Mustafa Kemal after war. Your leader has refused to sign Sevres treaty while ours signed the Versailles. We left our Baltic port Danzig to Poland. They further humiliated Germany by leaving Alsace Lorain to France. But no one is hopeless now, since we have a leader like Mustafa Kemal and he is Adolf Hitler. Our führer reminds us our real enemies France and Britain. We learn the facts about the Jews who sucked our blood over the years. I am very proud of the young Germans who take oath to change the picture in Europe, to create a different Germany in the future. At night, Husein thought Gabi's words. Hitler and Mustafa Kemal were incomparable. Hitler was sowing the seeds of hostility even in peace. Kemal declared war as a murder, if homeland was not at stake.

The first thing he did after independence war, was to initiate Balkan pact among the one time enemies.

Two days later Husein went to the registration office in the university. The moment he told his name to the officer, she was excited. Suzy, Turkish student came who is the guest of Frau Gabi. Less than a minute, officers finished his registration and wished success to him. One month after Husein started the classes, he had a lot of friends from all circles. He realized that the wealth of German people was not as enviable as he was told before coming to Berlin. All his friends were living in much smaller houses than Gabi's. They had to work in a job after school hours, till late times in the nights. Once, in a night club, he met a girl from his class, working as waiter. Unfortunately they had been made believe that the reason of their poverty was the Jews. Some Germans with common sense, never believed in that but could never talk either.

In November 1932, elections held in Germany. Hitler's Nazi party won the elections winning 196 members in the parliament. It was not enough to form the government. Hitler agreed a coalition and was declared by Hindenburg as the prime minister of Germany on January 30, 1933. When parliament building was burned Hitler accused communists and got the full authority from parliament to run the country. After Hindenburg death, with a referendum

Germans elected him both president and prime minister in 1934. Upon collecting all authorities in himself, he founded Gestapo and built the concentration camps.

Husein was sorry and confused. He regretted to come to Germany. One week-end, he went to cinema with his friend Moiz. On return they found the mother of Moiz, was crying.

In their absence Moiz father, had been taken by Gestapo. Moiz also started to cry when he saw a multiplication mark on their gate. Husein tried to console them.

- Don't cry Aunt Rachel. The daughter of my land lord, is a high ranking officer in a youth camp. She can know where your husband is.
- Don't do it Husein. Then you are registered among the suspects. They destroy your life.
- But what will happen to Moiz? How he will continue his education?
- My education is finished to-day my friend. From now on my mother and I, have to run away from Gestapo. If not we find ourselves in concentration camps.
- What kind of places are those camps?

- They have been invented by Nazis to find cheap labor force. You work in the hardest conditions as long as you can endure. Once you are exhausted you are sent to poisonous gas chambers. So my father went to a road of no return.
- Do you have food for dinner Aunt Rachel?
- No Husein. All our money was in the pocket of my husband and gone with the Gestapo.

Husein had recently drawn his allowance, remitted by his father. He was not in need of money near Hans Peter's family. He gave most of his money to Moiz, who went out to fetch some food.

Minutes after Moiz left, the door was knocked. The man at the gate was Professor Franz Sticher from Berlin University

He was the closest friend of Rachel's husband. While he was listening Rachel, Moiz came with food packs.

- You say they took Salomon to the camp. What are you going to do now Rachel?
- I don't know Franz. If Moiz can save himself, the rest is not so important for me. It will be better even if I die quickly.
- I don't go any place without you mom. If you will die, we shall better die together.
- Wait my neighbors. Don't be so pessimistic.

- Franz what kind of hope can we have? If our Turkish friend Husein had not helped us, we could die from hunger.
- Look friends. Germany made an agreement with Turkey.

Mustafa Kemal asked 600 professors from Germany as to lecture in new universities he opened in Turkey. Nazis Agreed upon, both to get rid of us and to continue good relations with Turkey. My name is registered among the candidates. The clerk in the office, is one of my old students. I can register Moiz as my assistant.

- If you can do this Franz we shall be obliged to you.
- What will happen to mom Uncle Franz?
- Don't worry about me Moiz. You save yourself.
- No Rachel? I thought all of you. You divorce Salomon and marry me. Then come with us as my wife.
- Do you think we can get visa from Turkish embassy?
- Turkish ambassador Mr. Necdet Kent, is such a kind man that he saved so far the lives of hundreds Jews this way. They put their plan into implementation. In short time Mr. and Mrs.Sticher were on their way to freedom with their son Moiz. But the remaining ones were hopeless. All they could do, was to wait the time of death in gas chambers.

Husein thought many times to go back to Turkey. But his teachers and friends in the school were so nice to him he had nothing to complain. Besides German economy was in the boom. Unemployment problem had been solved. He knew that if he had interrupted his education he would not have any other chance to complete it. 1936-1937 term was the last one of his education. One day in school he met Marlen, who was in the class, one year below him. She had lost her parents and raised by her uncle. Their relationship turned to a passionate love shortly.

Helga was aware of the change in Husein who opened his affair one day to her.

- Aunt Helga. I will be graduating this year, yet don't know what to do? Everybody will be waiting for me in Turkey. But I do not want to leave Germany because I love Marlen. She has one more year to finish the school.
- Do you think to marry her? If you do, will you take her to Turkey with you? Does your father know your relationship?
- I cannot think of a life without Marlen. I want to marry and take her to Turkey. But I am hesitant to inform my dad.
- One cannot always find great loves like yours. Be aware of its worth, not to feel lifelong regrets. Never leave Marlen, Husein. After graduation you can easily find job. Get a job to work one

more year in Germany till Marlen will also finish her school. Then marry her and immediately go to Turkey. The future of Germany does not look bright.

- Don't you think my father will be angry?
- Never will be. Just the contrary he will be proud of you for achieving something, we could not do.
- Did you love my father aunt Helga?
- Ours, was a great love too. We could not live even one day without meeting. Unfortunately he was married before our relationship. You and Marlen do not have such a problem. So nothing should be able to separate you.

Husein, listened to Helga. He decided to wait Marlen's graduation patiently.

In 1936, Hitler occupied Alsace Lorain which had been taken away from Germany and given to France. All treaties from Word War I, were being torn off. Germans were crazy like drunken. They were all confident for the future with the ever growing economy and unbeatable military power.

Husein found a job easily in 1937, with the help of Gabi. He was assigned as a controlling engineer in the development ministry, in charge of construction of the infrastructure. He had become the favorite employee of the minister, who was the successful man of Hitler. Husein was on the way to inspect a building construction, together with his assistant Wolff. They were in a place looked as prison to Husein. In the hall there was space, enough at least for 100 people to sleep. Husein wondered, why there was only one toilet and no wardrobes and tables in such a big space. Then they entered another big hall with no window and doors, except a narrow hole. But heating could be provided perfectly with huge gas burners on the walls. Hasan appreciated very much, what he thought garbage burning ovens, to get energy. On the way back to Berlin he told these deficiency and perfections to his friend. He exclaimed a lot.

- What do you say Husein? That was not a prison. It was the gas chambers where non-productive jews are sent to hell.

Husein could not sleep that night. He recalled, how Moiz and Rachel were collapsed in hopelessness when their father was taken away from home. He revolted Lord's justice. How could he permit the sufferings of poor men and empower of the cruel ones, to act so inhumanly. He thought to go back his country. But what would happen to his angel face Marlen then.

The year 1938 brought big changes in Europe. Hitler annexed first Austria and then Czechoslovakia. The victors of World War I, could not show any reaction. It was not important for

Husein. Marlen had received her diploma. They met in a restaurant to celebrate her graduation and review plans to return Turkey. But Marlen had no face of happiness or the joy of graduation in her manners. Husein asked.

- Why you look sad Marlen on a day should be your happy one. In less than a week we shall be free in Turkey.
- I am sad Husein for my obligation to leave you forever.
- Why do you talk like this Marlen? I bought our tickets.
- My life was destroyed Husein, at just the time I had hopes of life long happiness with you. They took me to a youth camp after giving my diploma and forced me to a sexual intercourse with a German military officer, to bring a pure German generation into the world. I disgust myself and ashamed of looking at you.

Husein was shocked with what he heard. He could not say anything. Marlen had been raped forcefully beyond her control. Has her heart lost its purity with the stolen virginity? Should he put an end to the love of his life? She had not asked any excuse nor request for being forgiven. Just the contrary she tried to protect the honor of her lover by sacrificing her life. Husein answered her.

- No darling nothing has changed in our program. We marry tomorrow and go to Turkey the day after. We shall leave the tyranny in Germany to create our heaven in Turkey.
- Don't do it Husein. What if, I may have to give birth to someone else child?
- Marlen, mothers carry their children in their wombs but fathers carry them in their hearts. Whoever may be borne by you, it is human kind to be my baby too.

Marlen, looked at Husein with amazement, admiration and obligation. It was a stare, comprising too many feelings, no language could properly express.

19

KING EDWARD
VISITS TURKEY

King of England, Edward VIII visited Turkey in 1938, to see Ataturk whom he admired. Ataturk met him at Istanbul Dolmabahche port personally. After the dinner they sat in one of the big rooms of Dolmabahce palace. While sipping their coffees. Edward turned Ataturk.

- His Excellency please call me Edward.
- I want you Edward to call me Kemal then.
- I read your conversation with General Mc. Arthur Kemal in 1933, about the fate of Europe. All your predictions, are coming true. How could you be so precise?
- With the knowledge of history and common sense Edward.

I always believed the people like us, should predict the facts beyond the horizons. So I told general Mc. Arthur that Germany have been imposed, unbearable conditions by force, as Versailles treaty. A nation like Germans, will never tolerate such a humiliation. Now French people regret Versailles treaty and is ready to sacrifice Alsace Lorain, if Hitler stops there. You did the same to Greeks. You encouraged them to occupy west Anatolia. They thought they would reestablish Byzantine Empire. When you stopped your support, they realized who they were.

- What can we do with Germans Kemal? We gave them all they wanted.
- They got all they wanted. But you have not mended their dignity. It will only be mended if they occupy all Europe.
- You mean they can start a war?
- I guess they will start the war till 1940.
- But that will be disaster Kemal. Will USA join the war?
- At a later stage. Yes.
- Can you also tell me who is going to win the war?
- Not you Edward, neither Germans, but Bolshevik Russia.
- Will Turkey be joining the war Kemal?
- Never. If the homeland is not at stake, war is a murder.
- You do not feel bad about that we forced you to WW I?
- No Edward. We reconciled our problems in Lausanne. Let me predict you one more thing. Among the all treaties made in 20th century, only Lausanne will turn to 21st.

- How do you think Turkish people feel about Britain?
- Let me tell you an old Turkish proverb. Our ancestors said.

"If you are going to hang yourself, use British rope."
We always preferred an honest enemy to dishonest friend.

- Frankly speaking Kemal do you truly not feel bad, for the loss of Syria, Iraq, and Palestine? Have we reconciled our conflicts on oil fields in Mesopotamia for instance?
- Frankly speaking Edward, you did us a great favor, not short but in the long term, by lifting the bloody Middle East conflicts over us. But those people who betrayed Turks, their 400 years old friends, made the greatest disfavor to themselves. They will be regretting before the turn of the 20th century. Last but not the least, I want to make another prediction Edward. There will be one day after 100 or 150 years when oil reserves will be running short. I believe human kind will invent alternative energy sources to replace oil. But laziness of oil rich countries will never be replaced by inventiveness of the modern societies.
- Kemal I want to confess, what motivated me the most, to visit you. I read your April 25, 1935 speech on the occasion of 20th years of Gallipoli. If you had not accomplished any of your achievements

and only told these words, you would still be my favorite leader in the history. Any commander in the history who won the Gallipoli victory would praise his own soldiers. You do just the opposite.

"English, French, Australian, New Zealand, Indian heroes"

- You speak about Turkish soldiers, not for discrimination but for equalization.

"There's no difference for us between Johns and Mehmets. Rest in peace under the soil of a very friendly country"

- Who would remember the mothers of enemy, except you?

"You the mothers who sent your sons to far away countries wipe off your tears."

- But your most striking words Kemal, came at last which still made me cry, when I recall.

"Having lost their lives in this land they have become our sons as well"

- I thank you for your appreciation Edward.
- What do you think about the future of India Kemal?
- In 15-20 years' time, two even three independent states will emerge from India Edward. Not only India, but in Africa as well, you will be losing most of your colonies.
- How can you be so sure Kemal?
- By initiating the fall of Ottoman Empire, you prepared your own destiny, either. Ottoman Empire was dominant on lands and you were dominant on seas. Our fall, will serve as an example, on you. Our War of Independence will be driving force, in the battles against your colonialism.
- Kemal, I was watching and admiring you from a distance. But my appreciation was many folded after I met you. If English and Turkish people had not been opponents in World wars our countries would be better than today, would they not?
- I confirm your thoughts completely with one addition Edward. Not only our countries but the whole world might be more peaceful in the future. Those who helped the confrontation Britain against Ottomans, in reality have been the enemies of humanity.

20

WORLD WAR II

In Hitler's Germany everybody was extremely delighted at the beginning. Austria and Czechoslovakia were annexed with not major objection from other countries. The left bank of Rheine was occupied to mend the broken dignity of German nation. Some people with common sense were not comfortable with the pressures imposed on Jews but they could never openly tell. Because the majority of public were convinced that the past deprivations were caused by Jews versus the recent prosperity. But there were some eager people not satisfied with the public content, like Hitler himself and his staff.

- My valuable friends. In the past five years till to-day we succeeded incredible achievements. Should we stop here? No German will answer this positively. Danzig is still a wound in our heart. Imperial powers drew maps after the war and gave the territories which were won by blood, to their allies at no cost, by humiliating the actual owners. It is an intolerable crime that what they did to us is the same of what they did to Ottomans. Now it is our time to revenge. We shall strengthen our military, by tanks and war planes and attack like lightning to get back our land from Poland.

- Heil Hitler. Dear führer your plan is clever as always. But we all know that Russians also have ambitions on Poland.

If we confront with them in Poland we may have some troubles on other frontiers.

- You are right my general. I declared communism as one of our greatest enemies. But in order to achieve our goals, we may cooperate with them at the beginning. I shall send my foreign affairs minister to Moscow and try to come to an agreement with them to share Poland between us. This way none of the Europeans can object our occupation.

- Heil Hitler. You are very clever my führer.

After this meeting, German Russian pact was signed on August 23, 1939. German tanks entered into Poland on September 1, 1939. The deed to share Europe was in effect irreversibly. Soviets occupied Finland on March 2, 1940.

Germans occupied Denmark and Norway on April 9, 1940.

Holland and Belgium in May. In June 1940 they marched in Paris. German dignity was humiliated by

Versailles treaty had now been mended. Russians followed the trend by invading Romania on July 1940. It happened a kind of intercontinental race between the offensives. Italy had eye on North Africa and Japan wanted to have territory in Asia. Germany continued her act in 1941, by entering first Greece and then Yugoslavia.

Hitler calls his staff.

- My valuable friends. Today is May 1, 1941. Germany has finished the task in Europe. If we had been a weaker nation we would satisfy with what we acquired. But no. You cannot stop such a disciplined army when on march to win. As long as our greatest enemies Britain and communist Russia stay in the world, our task is unfinished. Now I shall give you important news. Marshall Rommel is on the way to Africa with our powerful panzer tanks squadron to give the Britain the lesson they deserved. Another German army will march into Russia next month. I want you to tell me your opinions openly.
- Heil Hitler. My führer as you know my father was a German general who fought against allied forces, with Ottomans. One day he told me an interesting thing about geo-politic. He said that the long term superiority of the nations to each other, was dependent on two things.
- Did your father say technological superiority?

- No my führer, he said. The size of the land and the number of population. No matter how superior an army can be, as they advance in a vast land, they lose integrity and power.
- What do you mean general?
- I mean my führer. Russia is too big to control by a limited number of soldiers. Even if we advance at the beginning by a surprise attack, as long as we spread over a larger area we shall lose our strength. Let us not repeat the same mistake Napoleon did. The same thing can apply to North Africa as well. Britain is the dominant power on seas. They will have no logistic problem as we might face. Let us not repeat the same mistake of what Ottomans did. Let us keep and sit on our acquisitions at least 10 years and wait for the normalization of the political environment.
- You may be right in your historical examples general. But you forget two things. First; we are superior now on land by our panzer tanks, on seas by our U submarines and in the air by Luftwaffe plains. If we wait for some time, we may be losing this superiority. We may have even lost the territories we gained in Europe. Second; you forget my friend, is the geniality of Adolf Hitler. We should also give lesson to Britain which crashed us in WW I.
- My führer, I may accept to give lesson to all Europeans. But what we have anything to do with Russia? Have we not made a non-offensive

pact with them? Have we not shared Europe with them? Instead of giving lessons to others why don't we take lesson from Napoleon for instance?

- Gentlemen don't forget your promises to obey me. Remember, some of you criticized my Jewish policy as well. But now you and German people realizes how our prosperity developed in short time.

In the meantime, the prime minister of Japan holds meeting in Tokyo with high ranking commanders and politicians.

- Gentlemen, have you seen what Hitler did, in three years?

He owned most of Europe. Now they reach North Africa and west Asia. We are delaying in the race of sharing the world.

While western countries will have problem with Germany, we should fill the vacuum in the Far East.

- General speaks very much the truth my prime minister. What England, France and Holland got anything to do, in Philippines, Sumatra, Borneo and Java?
- Japanese army is fully disturbed with this injustice my minister. Look at the size of Australia

under British dominance and check the distance between two countries.

- My dear friends. I would also share your opinions if there had not been a slight problem. Can, what we plan in Pacific Ocean, disturb our trans-oceanic neighbor USA?
- We can never ignore USA. But we should have learned from Germans, what to do in such cases. It is to paralyze the enemy with a surprise attack.
- Do you mean to attack on USA naval base in Hawaii?
- Why should it not be? If USA puts a barrier, we lift it.

Just at this time there is a cabinet meeting in Rome, chaired by Mussolini.

- You see what Hitler did in three years. He owned most of the Europe. If he annexes Russia as well, our friend Hitler will not leave anything to us. Are we not, the descendants of Roman Empire?
- My esteemed Duce. Last year we tried to occupy Greece but failed. What can we get in Europe, Hitler took all?
- Africa my general Africa. The continent is both close to us and has natural resources.

Prime Minister Ismet Inonu holds a meeting in Turkey.

- Gentlemen, Germany became neighbor after occupying Greece. What kind of actions do you think?
- My esteemed president. Don't we have a non-offensive pact between Germany? Do you think Hitler attacks us?
- Hitler had the same agreement with Russia. But as you saw he disregarded his words. I think we should stock food reserves for our army, in case of need.
- My president, neither our budget allowances permit to make stocks nor our grain on the fields suffice to cover the food need of the people, in case of an emergency.
- To protect the people from starvation we distribute the main needs by limited quantities. If our budget does not permit, we collect taxes from rich people. We may leave them without food but not without fathers.
- In such case my president, we must unload Kurtuluş cargo ship we loaded food to help starving people in Greece
- You should neither stop shipping food to the needy now, nor in the future. I prefer to feed my people half sufficiently in Turkey, rather than ignoring the starving children in the neighbor.

21

HUSEIN'S LIFE
IN TURKEY

In July, 1938 Husein and Marlen got on train from Berlin. They passed all the way from German occupation areas. They were fearful in each control. Turkey and Germany were friendly countries and no serious problem arose. Marlen was also enjoying from Turkish immunity as the wife of Husein. At last they arrived at Gallipoli and embraced by parents, Ali aga and Zeynep. Fatma, the first wife of Ali aga had passed away. As Helga had predicted, Ali aga had been extremely happy to meet Marlen. He had loved his daughter-in-law at first sight.

Marlen has got used to Gallipoli very easily. There were no asphalt streets here, but people when walk on sand and walk in the fields with bare foot they were getting rid of their stresses. There were no municipal parks. But the people were living here in open nature, more healthy than man made recreation areas. In Germany factories were illuminated with artificial light. In Gallipoli there was sun light all around. During Hitler years nobody could trust the closest relative or neighbors. Here there weren't any untrustworthy persons. Villagers used to approach, not humans but even animals, with love. Marlen found the same hospitality everywhere. She could never be able to pay for any service or goods she purchased. Gallipoli was like a heaven where earthly payment means were not valid.

At last she realized her pregnancy which brought great joy.

The news from Germany were not so good. Germans had advanced to Moscow, but had been stopped there. Marshall Montgomery had defeated German's panzer squadron of Rommel, in El alameyn, North Africa. Divine tragedy had been repeated and Germans faced the same destiny of Napoleon. Those wished to leave a glorious mark in history would be recalled as the characters of big failures.

Turkey had not entered the war but there were no single family member, who had not suffered from deprivations of war. Black market was a usual practice especially in food purchases. Rich merchants of Istanbul were visiting Husein to buy his rice and wheat crops on the field at double of the market price. He asked time from traders to discuss it with his father. Next week some others visited and offered triple of the market price for dairy products. Germany was exhausting.

% 80 of the cities and production facilities were demolished. Husein knew that after war, engineers like Marlen and himself would be favorite ones. But there were time to those days and still they need money. So he sold all his crops at triple of the market price without informing his father. He was sure that if he had sold at normal price, the merchants in between would put the difference in their pockets. This period of nice profits would last 3 years.

Marlen's birth was nearing. In October, 1942 they came to Istanbul one week before the expected time. They hired a hotel room close to the hospital. During the week, Husein showed Marlen the sightseeing of Istanbul. At last the time has come and Marlen gave birth to a beautiful baby boy. They returned to Gallipoli victoriously. Ali aga named the new born, Hasan junior after his uncle. From the very first days of crawling, Ali aga has been the great lover of Hasan junior. He could only sleep in the arms of his mother and grandfather. His happiest moments were those he used to ride on his grandfather's back. After walking Ali aga used to take him to the shore where Hasan junior could swim only if grandfather was near him. Ali aga had lost one son but gained one grandson.

Towards the end of 1944, the family had gathered in the garden to celebrate the second birthday of Hasan junior.

While he was running in the garden a rusty iron nail was stuck in his leg. Marlen could hardly stop his crying. He then puffed out two candles on the cake. Three days later he was burning in fever, in his bed. Husein took his son to Gallipoli military hospital. Doctors diagnosed tetanus. Unfortunately in war conditions, at nowhere they could find necessary medicine and serum. The little boy died in screams. Ali aga was so sorry that he did not want to live after his beloved grandson. As a matter of fact, he could not. He passed away after a stroke.

Marlen and Husein had run away from the cruelty of Hitler but could not find happiness in Turkey. Husein had lost his father and son in three days. Nothing was consoling him. He used to cry sometimes long minutes in his bed.

One night Marlen embraced her husband

- Husein don't cry my love. Everything passed
- No Marlen. I could not forget anything. I revolt to my god. Why Lord only destined sufferings for us?
- I asked the same question to myself several times Husein.

I revolted first when I lost my both parents in an accident. I asked the reason why when I learned the death of my Jewish friends in gas chambers. Those sinless human beings had also been created by the Lord. Why did he not prevent them against murders? I could not find satisfactory answers to these questions. I was thinking that there could not be more tragedy than what I lived in Germany. I learned in Turkey that losing one's son was the greatest torture could ever be imagined.

- I asked the same questions myself Marlen. What hopeless thing to be a human. Look at the world after the war. Forty million died with no cause. They had the same pain like us.

They also had to leave their friends, relatives and children.

I have no trust in divine justice. The Lord who gave the way to Hitler, must be the cruelest among us. I want to commit suicide to express my revolt against God.

- No Husein. You cannot leave me alone, with our unborn baby. Then you will too be among the cruelest ones.

Husein looked at his wife unbelievingly. No she was serious. He could not think of anything and started to cry.

He had woken up to a new climax. The world was changing too, not to experience bed old days, in the future. There were attempts to found United Nations with the declaration of human rights. A new financial system was set up as the World Bank and IMF. At last Marlen gave birth to baby girl.

With her golden hairs and blue eyes she was as beautiful as angels. They named her Peri. She had been the remedy to her parents and grandmother to forget their sorrows

22

DIVINE TRAGEDY

On February 2, 1943 German army enslaved by Russia in front of Stalingrad. Italy followed Germany in retreatment.

Allied European armies, under the leadership of USA, occupied Sicily on July 10, 1943 then entered Naples on October 1. The last standing of Germany was in Monte Cassino. They could hold the lines for few months till May 17, 1944. After crashing Germans in Italy, allied forces planned the last strike and landed Normandy on June 6, 1944. Hitler was in his shield with his sweetheart Eva.

- Adolf, you caused the death of so many young people and finally Germany lost all the gains. Was it worth to lose the lives of so many young men, by so much ambitions?
- I loved my country and people too much Eva. The purpose of my fight was to make Germany the master of Europe.
- Extra patriotism does not always mean to be useful to a country Adolf, like your ambition did not yield the benefit you dreamed of. Look at young Turks on the last days of Ottoman Empire.

They started with patriotic goals at the beginning. But after a while Adolf, your kind of people starts loving themselves more than their country. They wanted more, to print a mark in the history, on account of thousands lives, rather than the well-being of their country.

You have been the worst of all ambitious human beings. You did not know to stop when you occupied the whole Europe. Unnecessarily you challenged Russia and Britain.

You underestimated USA. At last you took your lesson.

- You are right Eva. I underestimated USA. But I don't mean to underestimate their military might. Our scientists were about to invent a nuclear bomb. I could not think that Americans would kidnap our scientists working on this project. If Germany had invented the atomic bomb earlier, no one could resist against us.
- Adolf, 40 million people have died so far in a war you initiated.

If Germany had invented nuclear bomb would you agree to kill another forty million. May be only because of this, God did not make you successful.

- Eva, you criticize me just because I have not achieved my goals. If, Americans one day build this weapon, do you really believe that they will not use on humans? If the Jews, I killed now, would have opportunity in the future, will they act more humanly than me, on their subjects. Do you really believe that my opponents now, will be more civilized than me if opportunity arises? French people who were saved from occupation by Americans. Do you think they will be thankful to their saviors in the future or ignore them saying don't stick your nose into European affairs? I am afraid if Europe gets into trouble in the future they will again ask help from America. Because ignorance, ungratefulness and untimely courage are divine tragedies will humiliate human kind as long as they live.

It did not take too long over this conversation American and British forces entered into Köln on March 7, 1945 passing Rheine River from Oppenheim and Wessel. On April 20, 1945. American and Russian troops were marching on Berlin to divide the city between themselves. Hitler got married to Eva Braun, to do at least something good in his last moments waiting his end in the shield.

- I am sorry Eva. I could neither give happiness to you, nor to my country. I wish I had failed and died at the beginning.

I wish I could save the lives of 40 million people.

- Don't over blame yourself Adolf. When German people and I followed, you were the one who made our dreams come true. If the divine tragedy had been our divine destiny nobody would prevent it. Now finish your last task. First shoot me and then yourself to close down the curtains.

Germany surrendered on May 8, 1945. The war in Europe had finished. But Japan was resisting in pacific. Churchill left London to go to a place nobody knew. Next day he was with President Truman in white house.

- I came to thank you and USA Harry, both on account of Britain and Europe. If you had not helped, Europe today would be a state of German empire.
- You can share the same pride Winston. Are you not half American from your mother side.
- Thanks Harry, by joining our forces we defeated Germans.

But I cannot feel the full pride unless we defeat Japan as well. You know recently they bombarded Darwin Australia and we could not do anything.

- Can you keep secrets Winston? If I had not thought of criminal accusations, I would force them to unconditional surrender in one week.
- Don't tell me you invented nuclear bomb, Harry?
- Oh. I see you know too much.
- You know Harry, our intelligent service works well.
- Yes Winston. Scientist we kidnapped from Germany succeeded to separate particles and liberate the energy holding them together.
- I am happy to know this Harry. That means we solved Japanese problem.
- I have not yet decided Winston. If we use this bomb we shall kill thousands of innocent men and women.
- If we do not use it, thousands of American and British men and women will lose their sons. Development of Europe and the world will be delaying for years.
- You speak nice Winston. But what sin Japanese people committed to be victim?
- Divine tragedy destined them to be Japan. You know the wild nature rules. If you are strong, no one calls you murderer but hero. You are even supported by the historians. If you are weak you are blamed as criminals without a court verdict.
- I do not understand Winston. Why we have, then criticized Hitler? What was his difference from us, in cruelty?

On August 6, 1945 first atom bomb exploded on Hiroshima. 140000 innocent people were killed without discrimination of young and old, women and men. Second came three days later over Nagasaki which caused the death of 80000 people. It took only another three days for Japan to agree unconditional surrender with USA.

On September 1. World War II was over.

23

POST 1950 DEVELOPMENTS IN TURKEY

The year 1950 brought considerable changes for Turkey and Husein's family. With the general elections held on May 14, the ruling party has lost the election. By the land slide victory, newly formed Democrat party had won the majority seats in the parliament. Single party era was closed and the new government put liberal policies into implementation. The huge change, made Turkey among the eligible Marshal aid receivers together with Greece. Husein predicted the possible consequences very well. The new era would be the time of developments and constructions. To catch up the time was impossible by continuing as a farmer in Gallipoli. Next year his daughter Peri would start the primary school. He was ambitious to send her to a good school. He rented a house in Machka and family moved to Istanbul in fall. Husein formed an engineering and development company with his wife. He assigned Halil, the son of Salim aga to run the business in Gallipoli.

In 1951 autumn, their daughter Peri started the primary school. At the same time their development company had finished the apartment building construction on the land they inherited from their grandfather. Apartment flats were sold in a short time. They invested almost all the money they gained to buy new lands, for future development projects. Turkey was progressing so quickly that if one had the proper land and an attractive architectural project, one could sell most of the flats during the construction stage.

Year 1956 brought new happiness to Hamidoglu family. Their daughter Peri had finished the primary school. Husein enrolled her to the American College for Girls. German was her mother's language. She had learned a fair amount of Turkish at school. It was a family tradition to teach the children two languages and graduate from a university abroad.

At the beginning of 1957 some young military officers were in a meeting. They all have imaginations broader than tales and ambitions deeper than the oceans.

- How do you see the situation in Turkey guys?
- Disaster, not only in the rural areas but even in the bigger cities of Turkey, conservatives are in power. The barefoot villagers of yesterday, declare superiority over the state, by claiming democracy.

- How long can we, the patriots stand against humiliation?
- What really annoys me is, none of us, as the real owner of the country, do enjoy the freedom as we used to. To suppress the conservatives is forbidden, to criticize them is anti-democratic. Shall we let Ataturk be disregarded?
- O.K. guys. Shall we just simply watch?
- Of course not. Untimely moves may be risky but waiting too long might be too late. We should wait for the proper moment. Let us organize secretly for some time and collect new members among the young people.
- I think that is a very good idea. This way we can have time to fix our strategies to overthrow Democrat Party.
- Say we did it. Who is going to replace them?
- Why not someone from military chief staff?
- They say some, has no experience to run the state.
- That is not important because we shall help them. Even if we succeed them, things will go better.
- I fully share this idea. Turkish Military should be ruled by young generations.
- O.K. friends. Should we not select one of us, as the leader of this movement?
- We all have the sufficient quality to run the leadership. Have we not friends? Let us think on this issue after suppressing the conservatives.

When all countrymen become secular, the rest will be easy.
- Are you not missing one point friends? You want to overthrow a party elected by the nation and then replace it with military, to suppress the nation. Is it not against democracy and human rights declaration which we signed?
- It may look so, at the beginning. But when we shall put everything into order we shall retreat. These meetings and plans of the young officers have been informed to the government. In the meantime Democrat Party has won another election. The joy of an election victory for the party unfortunately brought complacency, to take actions.

Democrat party leaders, with this negligence prepared their own fate. More importantly, after the May 27, 1960 military coup they paved the way to other military interventions on:

March 12 1971, September 12 1980, February 28 1997, and

April 27 2007. No military commander could foresee how much they harmed the country by their habitual coups.

If they had let the change of governments, be made by free elections country would not lose the greatest opportunities like being a full member to European Union in 1980's, prepare a civil constitution, complete economic progress to a higher level and reconcile with Kurdish citizens.

Fifties have been productive for Hamidoglu Development Company. Foreign Capital Encouragement law passed in 1954, encouraged many foreign companies to invest in Turkey. Hamidoglu Development Company has been the main contractor, for the construction of factory or office buildings of many German, British, American companies.

Soon after, they had been the favorite contractor of the public tenders as well. In the meantime a letter came from Jenny in USA made Husein's family extremely happy.

"My dear in-laws Husein and Marlen. After so many years, I received a letter from my niece Peri. I cannot explain how happy I have been to receive a letter of remembrance from one of my relatives in Turkey. I and John still recall the magnificent days we had in Gallipoli and Istanbul. My son Hakan took over our law company and is curious about his uncle and his cousin. My daughter Jeanne helps her brother in the office. They are both married now. Hakan's daughter Michelle is 19 and preferred law education to continue the family tradition. My grandson Michael, the son of Jeanne, is at the same age with Peri. I have been happy to know that she started in American college for girls. I do not know if we can survive that long but my children and grandchildren hope to meet you one day, in Turkey or America. With love from Jenny and John."

They immediately answered Jenny, to inform their feelings by hearing from her. Peri had been a regular pen friend of both Jenny's children and grandchildren. They exchanged photos many times. It was a dream for Peri to complete her university education in USA. With this new family connection, she knew that her dreams were closer to come true. In 1958 summer, Hakan came to Turkey together with his wife Laureen and daughter Michelle. They visited the old Hierapolis and Antioch together. They admired history, as to praise to all their friends in USA. In June 1959 John and Jenny came Turkey with their daughter Jeanne and grandson Michael. As they planned a longer visit their son-in-law George could not join them. They spent one week in Gallipoli to revive all their memories and show those heavenly places to their descendants. They joined a great west and south Anatolian tour covering Izmir, Pamukkale, Antalya, Alanya and Cappadocia. On their return they spent their remaining days fully in Istanbul. Peri and Michael had been very good friends during the trip, to last afterwards.

After 1959 Turkey went into a chaos by political agitations. Republican People Party which was in power since the proclamation of Republic in 1923, had lost 1950, 1954 and 1957 elections. 2nd president Ismet Inonu was the leader and had lost his temper after the third free elections defeat in 1957. He instructed his members of parliament to vote negatively any bill brought to parliament by ruling party, even if it was to the benefit of the country. Democrat party reciprocated this attitude by confiscating the assets of the main opposition party. They increased the pressure on press and freedom of expression. They were intolerant to any criticism as to hold people responsible without court verdict. This extreme measures created a lot of oppositions against them from jurisdiction, universities and press. Some young military officers were in a meeting in 1959.

- Friends the time is getting ripe for a military intervention we have been waiting for years.
- It has been very good that Prime Minister Adnan Menderes called the professors as black gown people. According to what I heard, he is interfering with the promotions of the professors as well. Should they not be promoted with objective rules?
- Of course they should. But that is not the whole story. The newly founded investigation committees are acting like courts to accuse and send the people into jails. When we come to power we shall treat the public with more justice.

- Gentlemen have you heard that some opponents disappeared from whom no one heard anything.

Country-wide discontent was constantly growing. At last the time has come and young military officers captured administration on May 27, 1960. Everybody was pleased.

There was a huge support of countrymen to the military.

Young officers were in a meeting to decide what to do?

- This is the brightest day for us. At last we have achieved our goals and overthrown democrat party. From now on we shall work hand in hand and elevate the country to the brightest days. We shall make our decisions jointly without claiming to chair. What should be our immediate actions?
- We should first attack on corruption.
- That is good but it will take time to prove corruption by court verdicts. We need to act quicker. If we wait that long our military intervention will be unjustified.
- That is true. I therefore suggest that we prepare our own list that whomever we suspect for corruption we register.
- I think we should prepare another list for our commanders as well. Whoever we can't work with, we should put on list.

- That is good friends. Let us come to the meeting next week. In the meantime I talked some law professors. They will prepare a report about how we can justify ourselves.

Same officers were in the meeting next week.

- I collected your lists and added up the figures my friends. You suggest to pension off 235 generals out of 272 in the army. You also propose to cut off 7200 military officers from the army. Was this not too much to explain. Were we not trapped, with the same instinct which we criticized the ruling party for years?
- It may be but we do it, for our patriotism from which nobody can doubt. Everybody knows we are men with no ambition. Now let us listen two law professors I invited.
- Gentlemen we wholeheartedly congratulate. You achieved a great job. The legal justification of revolution is only possible with a new constitution. This way you can be released from responsibilities.
- That is good my professor. Otherwise why we should be held responsible for something we did for patriotism? The puzzle in mind is; can any of our successors blame us?
- In order to prevent this you should agree in advance to hand over the power to civil administration at the shortest.

- In that case, will those who take over from us, not urge to get rid of us?
- That's why we put two Assemblies to our constitution.

Senate and House of Representatives. You know what? We included lifelong senatorships for you.

- You did an excellent job my professors. We shall be lifelong obliged to you.
- That is not so important friends. We did it for patriotism.

There is a minor problem however. In order to put this plan into implementation, we should avoid criticism. That is why we request you to pension off some professors.

- I don't think that can be a problem friends. Can it? We did the same in the army, for regulation and benefit of public.
- Thank you very much. We shall give you our list next time. The last we should remind you that, if you do not sue all ruling party members in court, you will never be justified.

Next week, professors brought their lists. They had marked 1402 colleagues who were laid off with no reason. Those who supported the military intervention woke up the cruel reality at the end. Military commanders who thought that the young officer's move was against the ruling party, had found themselves out of the army.

Democrat Party members were all put into jail in a Marmara sea island as to be heard by revolution courts. Prosecutors have prepared such accusations that in short time, people realized that they were cheated. Prime minister, Minister of Foreign Affairs and Minister of finance all executed by court verdicts. The settlement among revolutionist officers had not been finalized until the elimination of fourteen more officers which came as a sudden surprise. The revenge accounts were still unclosed. One morning two police came and took Husein to police station. Military administration now was investigating business people who were involved in tender engagements with the state. Husein did not come back home at night. Peri and Marlen tried hard to get some information but could not do. Peri immediately sent a letter to Jenny. In the meantime Husein was sued and decided to be heard with no arrestment. The day Husein came home they received the letter from USA.

"My dear niece Peri. We were all sorry with what happened to you. Once your father situation is known come to USA.

When military interventions start in a country, it continues endlessly. Because there will always be some ambitious officers encouraged by past stories. That means neither Turkey nor your parents will have a predictable future. I checked with the colleagues here and learned some vital details. Your father should liquidate all his belongings before coming. For American visa please see Mr. Peter Ford in the Istanbul consulate. As soon as you arrive here we shall solve the rest. With love from Jenny and John."

Husein was found not guilty in the court. He liquidated all his assets in short time. They moved to USA in the fall of 1961 before Peri's school started. They adapted their new life very easily. They bought a house in New Jersey very close to Jenny. Husein was fond of spending his time in the large garden of the house. Peri was attending the same school with her cousin Michael. They used to do their homework, together. They were so much helping each other that at the end of the term they passed their classes with A grades.

24

AMERICAN ADVENTURE OF PERI

The family entered 1964 in Jenny's house. The old woman was very sensitive in this family get together. She had survived a great sea accident with her son and safely arrived New York. Not long after she had collapsed with the martyrdom of her husband Hasan. She was doubtful to continue the law company after her father passed away. She had achieved to continue it after long struggles. She thought no one could replace her husband. But the Lord granted her a second chance just on the land where she lost Hasan. She had even chance for a second child and gave birth to daughter Jeanne. Two children from two husbands were in harmony to run their family business. Her last joy was brother-in-law Husein's move to New York with his family. Although she was happy with her second marriage, she was delighted to be close to the family of her deceased husband. She was happy that her son Hakan knew his father's family. She had everything to be happy in life but still had some wishes. She was dreaming to see the graduation of his grandson Michael from college in June. The last she prayed was to witness the marriage of Michael and Peri whom she admired after knowing her. She thought to die afterwards.

It was the spring time of 1964. Peri and Michael was chatting in the garden about the examinations. They would finish the same college in the same year. They had to decide which university they would attend after the college.

Similarly important was to decide with whom they would go to graduation ball. It was a college tradition for a boy to express his interest in the girl most probably he would share his life. Michael asked his cousin.

- Have you decided with whom you are going to ball Peri?
- I had some invitations but no decision. Did you invite any girl?
- Nobody yet.
- But why? Are you not late?
- You are right. But if I shall not go with the girl I dream, I better stay at home.
- But why Michael? Is she discouraging you?
- Just the opposite. She behaves me nicely.
- What is the problem then Michael?
- The problems are; she is more than a friend, she is like sister to me. She does not know that I have been secretly in love with her for long time.

I don't know how she would take my unbrotherly invitation?
- I still say, don't be late. She might expect your invitation. If you delay therefore, you may resent her.
- You are right Peri. Would you like to be my partner at the graduation ball then?
- No invitation would make me happier than this.

Graduation day came at last. There were generations in the ceremony. John and Jenny were the oldest ones. Husein and Marlen were next to them. The young boy and the girl were their grandchildren of whom they were proud.

This young girl and boy had reminded them their youth, with joys and sorrows, still the years of great expectations. Peri and Michael came home happy but tired. They were relaxing in the garden, woke up with the voice of John.

- Dear grandson Michael and niece Peri. You gave us great pride to-day. Jenny and I believe that you deserved a gift from us. We decided to send you any destination you would choose in the world, for a two week vacation. Talk between you and just tell us.

New graduates were in debate after John.

- Michael, I think we should select such a place not to be easily reachable from America.
- I think the same Peri. But it should be also a place where we could meet the people from different civilizations.
- Michael, tell me do I want too much? I also wish a place with cultural richness.
- Tell you what Peri. I brought some brochures from travel agencies organizing international tours. Let's take a look at them. They looked at the tours. They agreed on one, both meeting their expectation and seasonally convenient.

It was a Russian tour including Moscow and Leningrad.

They got on plane towards end June. They scheduled to arrive their first stop Leningrad at 8.30 P.M. Peri was not happy with the time table. She liked to see the city from the plane during the day light. When they announced the landing, she looked down from the window. It was day light and an amazing city under the air craft. She recalled bright nights of the northern Europe. She excitedly held her cousin's arm.

- Michael. Can you look down? You cannot imagine such a beautiful scene. There are many islands on a river and wonderful bridges connecting them.

- Have you seen Peri how big are the buildings with the courtyards in front?
- These magnificent buildings with the golden domes must be big cathedrals.
- They really are. Have you noticed the very large streets? They are too large for an old city. At last, they landed on airport. Their hotel was very close to St. Isaac cathedral square. They admired the temple in day light. But it was closed due to late hours of the day.

Next day after breakfast they marked on the city map the places they wish to see. Hermitage was very close. They walked there and found a long queue in front of the biggest museum of world with 3 million art pieces to be exhibited. It was constructed as the palace by tsarina Katherina.

She had not only ordered precious pieces to the art centers but also collected Greek frescoes, Byzantium icons, British silver ware, Chinese silk clothes, Faberge jewelry, Sevres and Wedgewood porcelains for the museum. The palace was an architectural masterpiece, with its colorful façade reflecting on Neva River. Their visit lasted the whole day. What impressed Peri and Michael the most, was the painters gallery of the great artists like Da Vinci, Raphael, Rembrandt, El Greco, Velazquez, Cezanne, Monet, Renoir, Degas, Van Gogh, Titan, Picasso, Matisse, Kandinsky.

When great Petro captured the city from Sweden in 18th century, he liked its location very much. He believed that in order to be a great empire, Russia should have ports opening to the oceans. Black sea on the south was an inner sea under the control of Ottoman empire. But the new city was both very close to Europe and also on the coast of the sea. Petro transferred the capital city from Moscow to St. Petersburg in 1712. He invited most talented architects to Russia to plan the new capital with its streets, parks, buildings, and bridges. Master artists worked on the decoration of the palace. His enthusiastic move to rebuild a new capital, followed by his successors and emerged a jewel among the European capitals. When Peri and Michael returned hotel they were tired but completely satisfied with density of art. Next day they took a city tour with a Kirov ballet performance in the night. They have been enchanted by the beauty of music, quality of choreography, performance of artists and over all ambiance of the theatre.

In the hotel they were thinking the art loving tsars who elevated the country to raise the biggest composers, famous novel writers and talented ballerinas in the schools like Kirov in St. Petersburg and Bolshoi in Moscow. Next day Peri and Michael visited St. Isaac cathedral. It was fantastic to look at the city from the terrace under golden dome. Inner decoration which completed in 40 years, was beyond the imagination. They went to Kazan cathedral with the columns in front. Resurrection cathedral with the incredible front decoration attracted their attention at once.

It was also an important place for Russian history where Emperor Alexander II, had been assassinated. Inside the cathedral was like a mosaic and painting museum of the Christian history. They were hungry and wished to go back a restaurant near the hotel. They entered an underground station and amazed by the frescoes and statues like in a museum. They went to bed early since next day they would fly to Moscow.

They took the train from Moscow airport to the city. They passed through the magnificent forests but saw very poor houses. Could Moscow urban area be so lousy? They recalled the beautiful Baltic coast from airport to Leningrad center. Their hotel was on one of the busiest streets in Moscow. They had dinner in a restaurant close to the hotel.

People walking on the streets were better dressed than Leningrad. The buildings were also bigger in Moscow but lack of the same architectural beauty. Next day they visited red square around which, there were tall walls between the people on the streets and elites in the palace. Two capital cities of Russian Empire were reflecting the difference between art loving and autocrat administrations. The founders of theatres like Bolshoi and Pushkin museum were also those who made St. Petersburg a temple of art in Europe. It was really amazing how the same people could display different behaviors at the times of different rulers. The country of Tchaikovsky, Rachmaninov, Korsakov, Tolstoy and Chekov, after 1917 revolution, had changed the name of radiant St. Petersburg to dull Leningrad.

It was a divine tragedy that the same things happened in Nazi's Germany. The people among whom the treasures of humanity were raised; like Wagner, Bach, Beethoven, Goethe and Shiller, had displayed racist behaviors to non-Germans. They hailed a murderer as führer just like Russia had declared the killer of Tsar Alexander II as the heroic patriot, denying their glorious past.

Peri and Michael was happy when they were back in USA. They had not only the opportunity to visit two influential capitals of Europe but also to compare different rulings.

They had not only witnessed the conflict between ideology and art but also they had explored their inner virtues. They were fond of love rather than hate and used to request rather than dictate. They had understood that their way of living would be merciful rather than disgraceful. They had finally learned that their love was not for a moment but for the whole life. They got soon married. Michael chose political science for university education. Peri started in academy of journalism.

Divine Tragedy

In 1966 Peri graduated from academy as a promising young journalist. She had an offer from the famous New York paper, before sufficiently enjoying her vacation. In 1967 she had been a well-known reporter in the country. In February, Chief Editor Roger called her to his room.

- Peri, in short time you have been a successful journalist known by many Americans. But I believe, you still work under your capacity. The only reason for that is; you did not have a good opportunity to test the limits of your talents. But now opportunity is here
- You made me excited Roger. What is the opportunity?
- Listen Peri, Of course you should have heard that Arab world is in the preparation of a decisive strike on Israel.
- I heard Roger that Egypt, Syria and Jordan gathering their forces with the support of Iraq and Saudi Arabia.
- You are absolutely right Peri. But my gut feeling tells me that there may be a lot of surprises in this attempt. That's why, I want to assign you to follow this venture. I believe this is the opportune time to prove your limits in your career of journalism.
- Oh my god. I am not yet experienced in international affairs Roger. I do not know Arabic. How can I succeed?

- You cannot know before trying, can you? Look Peri, experience is gained only by trying. How we shall see the capacity of young journalists, if we do not try them in critical cases like this? If you accept this assignment you will have three to four months to go to Middle East. You can learn basic Arabic, during this period. We then talk.
- If you permit me Roger, I want to ask my husband.
- I urge you too, to talk Michael. He is going to represent USA, in the future. The qualification of spouses in such positions is extremely important. I mean your assignment is an opportunity for him as well.

Peri, went to Egypt in May after a condensed Arabic language course. As an American journalist she met a lot of people. She found all Egyptian authorities very hopeful. They were openly telling her, their expectations.

- Peri Hanim. Cemal Abdulnasir sent us by God. When he nationalized Suez Canal, none of us was hopeful. But now this important water way is belong to us. When he started Assuan dam, no banker opened credit to us, to hamper the construction. Assuan dam now, is about to be completed.
- Do you think you have sufficient military power to win against Israel?

- He is guiding Arabs with great leadership. When Egypt, Syria and Jordan will attack from three frontiers, Israelites will run to the Mediterranean.
- You mean what Mustafa Kemal did after WW I, you will do the same, is it true?
- Exactly Peri Hanim. They have 265000 soldiers versus 306000 of ours.
- But can their arms be superior to yours?
- No Peri Hanim. We are superior in that respect as well. Israel had 300 war planes, and 800 tanks versus our 1000 planes and 2500 tanks.

Peri, went to Jordan where she found the same optimism.

- Peri Hanim. Arabs will not give the lessons only to Israel but western community as well, who so far cheated us. Our target is to annex Jerusalem and west bank. The rest is belong to Egypt and Syria.
- You mean you already shared the territory?
- That is the rule of cooperation.

Peri went to Israel in June, both to feel the pulse and witness the end of the war. There were news about Egypt to send troops of 100000 soldiers to Sinai. But the people in Israel was calm with full confidence in their army. In the early morning of June 5, Israel planes flew at lower altitudes, over Mediterranean without being detected by radars.

They made a surprise attack on Egyptian bases and destroyed 300 planes and main airports at first strike. The same day Syrian and Jordan armies lost their air might seriously. Allied forces moved their tanks into the dessert. But after losing air superiority this move did not yield any glory. Just the contrary they have been hunted by Israel planes one by one. In 6 days, Israel had gained Golan Heights from Syria, Sinai Peninsula from Egypt, the whole Jerusalem and West bank from Jordan. They had expanded their territory by three folds in just six days by German surprise attack tactics. But they knew to stop as contrary to what Hitler did. The rest would be gradual settlement of the territories. Arabs learned that the cooperation between the allies was not sufficient without coordination among the acting forces. Peri availed her experiences by writing a book in the shortest time. In the fall, her book was already among the best sellers. She had been a famous journalist which brought promotions in the newspaper.

At the beginning of 1968, winds of change were blowing strong in Czechoslovakia. Alexander Dubcek had won the first secretariat of Communist party against Novotny supported by Stalin. He was a confirmed believer of communism who had worked in militia at war time against Germans. He had been the Member of Parliament from 1951 to 1955, attended Political Sciences school in Moscow from 1953 to 1958. On January 5, 1968 he had reached the top of his career by becoming the first secretary of the communist party. Shortly after these developments chief editor Roger called Peri into his room.

- Peri we would inform your new assignment earlier but waited for graduation of Michael, who may wish to accompany you in Czechoslovakia. You will go there, feel the pulse of public and report us. We wait a separate article from you about Dubcek, the leader of liberalization. Who is he? What is he aiming for his country?

Peri, went to Prague with Michael in June. Michael had gladly joined Peri after his graduation, not only for fun but to prepare his doctorate thesis on east Europe unique case. The city was like a down-sized copy of Leningrad, with its unique architectural design with bridges, cathedrals, art collections and cultural level of the people. They found connections in universities. They talked students and the people on the streets. They realized that the young generation was fully supporting Dubcek for change. The older generation was willing to be free from Russian influence, but did not wish to lose the advantages of communism. In the Marxist system there were no freedom of expressions, but also no unemployment, no lack of medical care, no poverty in retirement age which was perfectly suitable for old people.

Young generations were ambitious for opportunities to have private cars, luxurious houses and travels instead of equal living standards. Both generations had one question in their mind. Would Dubcek be able to change the country, without getting into conflict with Russia?

It did not take too long to learn the answer. On August 20, 1968 Russian tanks passed the borders and entered into Prague. The difference of Dubcek appeared here. He asked his countrymen not to resist. He had prevented his country from a second Hungarian tragedy, but could not succeed to change the autocrat face of Stalinism into a smiling eyes of the democratic ruler. He wished to change communism with the wisdom of great Petro, but failed this time, hoping that the winds of change would blow off all obstacles one day in the future.

When they were back in the States in September, Michael was putting the last touches on his doctorate paper. Peri had devoted all her time on the book about the life of Dubcek. In the meantime they learned about Peri's pregnancy. White and Hamidoglu families were in a happy expectation. Knowing she would not have time after the birth, Peri finished her book before 1969. In February Peri's new book was in the market One month later, Michael won the title of a doctor. He applied Foreign Affairs department and received a positive answer from the office. In one month time, he had to move to Washington. In the meantime Peri's book, were in the third rank in the best-selling books. Marlen and Husein would not send their daughter alone to Washington. Husein bought a house near the Potomac river.

They all moved to Washington together to their new house.

Peri's birth was nearing. John and Jenny had already arrived Washington with their own car. Michael's parents, Hakan and his daughter Michelle came on July 19 by plane.

Two days later Peri gave birth to a healthy boy. Jenny was crying and thanking God at the same time.

- Oh my god when I came to the USA, I was alone with my son Hakan. I am grateful to you that you gave me a big family and I saw my grandson today. I would not worry if I die after this.

They were all happy at home. They were in front of T.V. instead of talking about the baby. Because that day was an exceptional one for the nation. America succeeded to send a vehicle to moon and an astronaut was about to set foot on moon the first time in the history of mankind which was being aired from the moon. Millions of people in the world watched Neil Armstrong who stepped on moon from the space shuttle and said.

- This is small step for a man but a giant leap for mankind.
- Hello Neil, hello Buzz. President Nixon was talking.
- Neil, Buzz. America is proud of you. You made the dreams of all Americans come true. While you look at the world from sea of tranquility, we feel more obliged to bring peace into the world, for scientific achievements be meaningful.
- Dear president. It is the greatest honor to us, to know that we represent the whole human kind here.

   Hakan asked
- Do you remember my friends? When Russians sent the first man to orbit, we were all feeling sorry and wondering how Russia did it before USA? How an autocratic regime could overcome the free world? If the regime, who shed blood in Hungary and crashed Czechs by tanks, had been more successful than free world, it would be a shame for all of us. Husein do you remember in those hopeless days of 1960, what president Kennedy had said?

   He had promised that, before the turn of the decade, America would send a manned vehicle to the moon and will show more progress than Russia.

- Of course I remember Hakan and I wonder what a nation Americans are, they even program the dreams. Who can stop you after this achievement?
- Only Americans can stop America. If we swell with our achievements and use our technological might to crash weak nations like Korea and Vietnam, instead of being impartial between them we may be weakening or ineffective to achieve our targets.

    Jenny interfered.

- Your political debates made us forget our new born baby.

    I suggest we name him Neil, in commemoration this exceptional day. Let us pray he should be as successful as Neil Armstrong.
    Everybody accepted Jenny's proposal with applauds.

    Next day, those visited by planes went to the airport. Jenny and John got on their cars to drive to New York. When phone rang, Marlen took the line. It was from highway traffic police. Jenny and John had lost their lives in a traffic accident. The family who was joyful with the birth of Neil was grieved with this unexpected loss. Michael revolted.

- My grandparents were extremely happy with the birth of Neil. Why my Lord took them away on such a day. Is this not a divine unjust Husein?
- It is difficult to understand this Michael. But one thing consoles me. Jenny wished to die herself. Do you remember what she said after taking Neil in her arms?

She said, "She saw the child of her grandson. She would not expect more than this in life" In my opinion Michael, we should not suffice with what we got in life. If we believe almighty Lord, we should always ask the best from him.

25

POST 1975 EVENTS

The year 1975 bought big changes for Peri and her family. With the assignment of Michael in Washington D.C. Peri had resigned from New York paper. But her book about nonviolent resistance in Czechoslovakia had not been forgotten. She called the editor of New York paper and asked if they would be interested in a new book about Turkey Greece conflict over Cyprus. The book was published in 1976 and became another best-selling book.

Second time in her career she had been successful. These achievements attracted the attentions in secretary of state. Michael had been assigned as deputy general consul in Istanbul as from mid-1976. The family was proud. For Marlen and Husein it was even more joyful as they had decided to come Istanbul with the family. Peri asked father.

- Daddy we are glad that you come to Istanbul with us. Will it not be difficult for you? Marlen answered.

- Of course it will be. But Neil is the most precious member of our family. How long can we love him after this age? Each moment we live with him is a plus for us.
- Thanks mom. Your contribution in raising our son cannot be forgotten.

Two months before Michael and Peri, Husein and Marlen came Istanbul with Neil. They moved one of the apartment flats they constructed. They enrolled Neil to Community School of American College. Three years passed with great happiness. It was quite cold in February 1979. Husein was at work and Marlen was alone in house. The doorbell rang. The old woman opened the gate and faced two young men with the masks in their face. The taller one introduced himself.

- We are from Turkish Communist party. We decided to kick out all aliens from the country for full independence. We know that you are German and son-in-law is American

We are decisive to take either your money or soul.

- Let's go to the drawer where I keep my money.
- Is that all you have? Do you cheat us old woman?
- If you want more, let us go to the bank. Then I can draw.

- We shall go to the bank and be caught by police.

The tall man after putting the money into his pocket shoot Marlen in the head. The old woman died right away. In those days these were the ordinary incidences in Turkey. No one was sure of the safety of life and money. When people or families were on streets, there can always be a fight between right and left wing supporters in which innocent people could die with an accidental bullet. Terrorists were financing themselves by stealing from public. In these robberies people were generally killed.

Assassination of Marlen was shocked everybody in the family. Peri collapsed with the untimely death of her mother.

- Michael I do not want to stay in this country any more. They learned we were Americans. We can always be exposed to these kinds of attacks.
- You know honey our house is under police protection.
- Then how did they kill my mother? I am more curious about our son Neil rather than ourselves. We cannot live in a country where people hate each other. Please ask your assignment. Daddy please come with us again.
- My Peri, after losing your mother I lost my joy to live. Look at the divine tragedy that I saved your

mother from Nazis in Germany and lost her to communists in Turkey. Like Jenny once said. I achieved all my targets, I found the love of my life. I had the prettiest grandson I could love. I want to die now and not to survive too long over Marlen.

Michael did what Peri said and got his assignment to Middle East desk in Washington. Family moved to capitol as soon as Neil finishes his school in June, together with their father Husein.

26

CHANGING WORLD

The year 1979, had not only changed the life of Husein and family but a lot of things in the world as well. In January 1980, Middle East desk was in meeting in Washington.

- Friends a lot of things changed last year in our area. Ayatollah Houmeyni overthrew the shah in Iran. Saddam Husein took control in Iraq. We have to elaborate new policies accordingly.
- We have to do this. Because you know new Iranian regime took hostage of 66 American citizens. We are ridiculed by many of our allies.

Michael interfered.

- Are we not partly responsible for this humiliation? Do you remember we had overthrown Prime Minister Musaddik just because he nationalized Iranian petrol? If we had not done it, shah could still be the ruler of Iran.
- Michael is right friends. American foreign policy is based more on maintaining present conditions rather than being proactive against the changing

world. Let us design a policy according to predictions in the Middle East in future.

- I think we can delegate Saddam to solve Iranian problem. He is both young and ambitious. If we support him secretly He would wish to prove himself. This way, we shall look not interfering Iran directly but make them bow before us.

- May I act as devil's advocate. Your plan is excellent if Saddam wins. What will happen if he loses? Don't forget his opponent will be 2500 years old Iran. What shall we do if Iraq resembles Greece in post-World War I?

- Do you mean Michael, Iraq may not be victor against mullahs, with all modern weapons we shall provide them?

- My parents-in-law lived in Germany during the World War II. They repeatedly told me one thing. If two countries encounter in a conflict, the most populous and biggest one wins in the long term no matter how small its military might be, like Hitler and Napoleon lost against Russia. We cannot compare the territorial size and population of Iraq with Iran, neither their historical depth.

- You may be correct Michael. But we shall equip Iraq with unbeatable weapons.

- Iraq may be superior to Iran at the beginning. But what happens if 100000 Iraqi soldiers spread over a 1.5 million square kilometer area. What is your plan, if Iran blocks the gulf passage to prevent oil transportation? We shall plant the seeds of animosity between Arab countries and Iran which is a bigger threat than we can strike with nuclear weapons. Last but the most important risk will be what, if Iran succeeds to manufacture their nuclear bomb.

- What else can we do? We are known as the defender of democracy. Instead of giving an image of intervening with administrations of other countries, is it not better to delegate the task?
- Why don't we try direct diplomatic relations? There is another issue to consider. What happens if Iran learns about our support to Iraq and turns to Russia which has occupied Afghanistan?
- If Iran had not taken our diplomats as hostage we would try dialogue with them. But now it is not possible.
- You mean what we did in Vietnam we shall repeat.
- Unfortunately such cases are hopeless ones. Politicians have to please public who elect them.
- But what we shall do if we have to tackle Afghan problem?

We shall probably support fanatic Muslims at the beginning who may kick out Russians from their land. But we can never guarantee that they will stay our friends forever.

As Michael predicted, fanatic Afghans had been the enemy of Americans as well in later years and had been the initiators of September 11 sabotage. Saddam failed in Iran and in order to gain his prestige he attacked Kuwait in later years. In 1985 Michael was appointed as the deputy consul in West Berlin. Peri was excited with this appointment although there were some difficulties. Once more they had to move their house. Neil was in his 16 and had to stay in USA one more year. At last they decided Neil should stay at home with his grandfather till graduation. Peri and Michael went Berlin one year earlier. In 1986 they too moved to Berlin and enrolled Neil to engineering school. Husein in spite of his old age was happy in Berlin. He had met some of his old friends and visited the places where he had some memories. But his happiest days were the fall of Berlin wall in 1989. Germans were one step closer to their great dreams with the unification of east and West Germany. It was the victory of liberalism against communism and democracy against autocracy. Husein had achieved all his goals. His daughter Peri had a happy marriage. He had seen his grandson as a young and successful man. He had met his old friends during the days but in the nights he was missing his wife Marlen. He was longing to meet Marlen and his son Hasan who could not spend much time in life. At the beginning of 1990 he was diagnosed cancer. He knew he had not much time in life. But he was not sorry. In life he had acquired all his wishes. It was the time to experience after world life if existed. It would be better to leave the world now in peace, instead of suffering the future pains.

27

FIRST LAYER OF THE AFTERWORLD LIFE

Husein had to undergo a serious surgery. They cut off part of his intestines. In the room of awakening, he recalled the beautiful days of his life. He should be grateful to God that he had memorable days. The biggest miseries of his life were the death of his son Hasan and the murder of Marlen.

He would feel happier if he had less benevolence in exchange for the lives of his son and wife.

Some weeks passed over the operation but he was not feeling good. His unbearable pains had started. Doctors checked him and found that there was a contamination of disease to other organs. They gave him some sleeping agents to make him feel less pain. It was such a tragedy that Husein was willing to die but surviving with pains. He wondered why God should destine such a painful end for him. He recalled a scene from a T.V. channel he watched. A newly born buffalo was being hunted by a lion and carried some distance between the teeth. How much pain and fear the baby buffalo should have felt? Husein was as much hopeless and painful as the baby animal, but at least had no fear of being torn. His daughter, son-in-law, grandson all were near him. Michael and parents had come from USA to visit him. Chemotherapy treatment had decreased his pains but left him so weak and tired that there was no difference between living and dying for him. So he had no fear of dying but longing to explore the afterlife realm.

One night, after falling asleep, a very bright light wakened him. His body was getting lighter and feeling to be ascending. He tried to look down. When he saw his body on the bed he understood that he had died. He recollected all his life and friends. He was still ascending and the light above his head was getting brighter. Once more he looked down. He saw the roof of his house. When he stared down the third time he was amazed to see the world as a globe from all angles. He then realized that his ascend was not linear but spherical as the electromagnetic waves, he had surrounded an area rather than watching a spot. He wondered how he was looking. Suddenly he felt himself as a smoke or a cloud. He had no eyes to see but a strange capacity to perceive. He had no physical mass but an energy field to cover a certain area. In his sphere of coverage, he recognized Mars and Venus. He recalled that NASA had organized some unmanned flights to Mars. The moment he thought of that scene he found himself on the surface of the planet.

Husein was exploring some afterworld realities. In life he heard from religious people that prophets like Jesus, Buddha and Muhammed, had ascended to the sky to reach the God. To the ministers, Lord was somewhere above, looking down the earth. Husein experienced that ascending meant to cover a larger area in the universe rather climbing a ladder. Cause no soul was needed wings, like the artistic depiction of the angels. Neither flying in the universe was possible. Wishing or thinking to be at a place was good enough for an astral voyage. Some privileged people might succeed this in life, which meant dissolution of physical body from mass to energy on earth and reversing the process on another space. Husein continued to observe Mars. There was not a friendly surface for human beings. There were big holes from different craters with no water and no green areas. Density of iron, had turned the soil to a reddish color. He was alone and missed the world. He wanted to be back on earth. But he could not succeed the astral voyage by thinking this time. He climbed a hill in Mars in front of him. He went further ahead. No one he could see either. Husein was in deep embarrassment.

Why had he not met his wife who had passed away before him? It was a burning experience not to see any of his relatives nor any human kind. Once more he wished to try an astral voyage. He thought to be in Venus. It was amazing this time the voyage had been achieved and he found himself in Venus. Although the heat had no impact on him, he could perceive the planet was hotter than Mars. The surface was similarly rough as Mars. Volcanoes were more eruptive here. There were dense sulphur smokes on the summits which was obstructing the sight. He was desperate in afterlife with the loneliness and unawareness of the future. How long this ordeal would continue to burn his soul without fire, torturing without hope. Why he was able to travel from Mars and Venus but unable to have a connection with the world. He thought to commit suicide as it would be possible in life. But neither cold nor heat nor anything else could damage the soul which had no mass. He wished to be in the sun. There were such high burning flames that he could not find any sight of sky. It was like to be in a universal prison where there were barriers without bars. Could this desperateness and loneliness within the exploding sun blazes all around, not be allegorically defined as hell, in the holy books? He questioned the Lord.

- My god what sin, I committed to deserve this punishment?

He recalled his good deeds in life. He had married Marlen, although he knew she was raped. He had saved her life by taking her out of Germany. He had given all his money to his neighbor Rachel, whose husband was taken to the camps. What did he get against his good deeds? God had taken his only son Hasan from him. Was this the divine justice? Right at that moment some images appeared on the screen of eternity from the life in Gallipoli. One of his loyal men was picking up seeds from the farm to find food for his pregnant wife. A woman was milking the cows in the night to feed her baby. Some fishermen was going out to fishing in the night to buy medicine for their sick relatives. Husein was sorry with these scenes. But he had excuses as well. He had not known any of them. But the images were changing rapidly. He saw himself talking to black market merchants. He was depositing extra money to the banks without informing his family. Right at this moment he saw his little son Hasan junior who was running in the garden. Husein saw him falling down and laying in the bed. It was enough for Husein to grasp the reasons of his punishment. He had exchanged the life of his son, with the undeserved money from black market merchants. His soul felt the greatest regret, no alive man could know. He knew there would be a price for his wrong doings on earth. He could not stay on the sun. Husein wished to break existing limits. He thought to be above the planets.

He found himself in the space over the Mars. There were thousands of rocks around him. He was in the asteroid belt between Mars and Jupiter. It was terrible to stay in the space beneath the falling rocks. He did not wish to go back to the planets he already visited. He thought to be on moon as the last resort. He landed on the surface of moon. He immediately saw the blue planet where he had been born, lived and loved. The surface of the moon wasn't any friendlier than the others, but looking at the world from a distance was worth everything. It was pleasing in utmost loneliness and encouraging in fierce hopelessness. He spent some time recollecting his earthly memories and beloved family members on the moon. He still prayed for forgiveness waiting for an indication of benevolence.

28

SECOND LAYER OF THE AFTERWORLD LIFE

At last Husein felt a strange desire. One more time he wished to be on earth. He prayed God for permission to visit home. A miracle took place right at that moment. He found himself in the garden of Berlin house. There were people whom he had not met at all. He then thought of their house in Washington. He saw a young boy practicing basket shots. His mother called him

- Nathan you must be tired. Come in and take a shower. Your father will soon be back. We shall decorate the year 2020 Christmas tree.
- Neil, darling. Dinner is ready. Get changed and come.

Husein was at loss. Could that man be his grandson?

Had it been so many years after passing away from the world? Where were his daughter Peri and son-in-law Michael? His soul made an astral journey to another destination. It was the American consulate in Telaviv. Michael was sitting behind a table as the General Consul of USA in Telaviv. A man came in his room.

- His Excellency. I have bad news for you. Your wife had lost her life, while she was in a shopping mall, after the attack of a suicide bomber.

Husein's soul was in a torment. Had his beloved daughter left the world? Had she shared her mother's destiny and become the victim of assassination. Had Marlen met Peri in afterworld life? Would Husein meet them one time in afterlife, or would he miss them eternally?

The scene had changed now. He saw some lousy buildings were under heavy fire. Men and women were trying to escape from burning buildings to save their children or old parents. In some other places children lost their parents were crying hopelessly. Husein had forgotten Peri. It was a greater multi fold tragedy where the people was exposed as the daily routine. He wondered why the almighty Lord was permitting these brutalities. Husein had been partly aware of the things happened in 30 years after his death. But he had no information about what he really wished to know. He prayed god in all his sincerity.

- Oh my god. You made me aware of the many events which took place in the world. But in a world of loneliness,

    I missed my wife, my little boy Hasan junior, my lovely daughter Peri and my parents. Is this a place of eternal loneliness and longing?

    I had heard in life that those parents lose their children in life would be rewarded by heaven in afterworld life. So far I have not seen any trace of the promised heaven.

29

THIRD LAYER OF THE AFTERWORLD LIFE

Husein found himself in the core of a bright light which took him to an unknown destination. When he felt to be landed, he perceived a beautiful ring of colors in the sky around a massive planet on the sky. He recognized the place from the school books. He should have been on one of the satellites of Saturn. For corporeal existences the surface could be considered cold but in spiritual world it would not mean anything. The second substantial object in the sky should have been Jupiter. The scene here was much different from the previous planets but the loneliness was same. He was about to complain that a human image appeared through the fog. He perceived some words.

- Welcome to the third layer of afterlife realm. My name is Suleiman. I'll be your guide in the subsequent journeys.
- But you are in human image.

- The souls reached this level can appear in any image they may wish.
- I am very delighted to meet you Suleiman. I had a lot of questions to ask. Can you tell me if I shall meet my family?
- You will meet them Husein but in further layers. How long does it take we cannot know. Besides, in afterlife realm, the concept of time is very much different from the earth.
- I know Suleiman. When I first saw the events in the world I was surprised to know 30 years passed over my death.
- What do you say? You must be a blessed supplicant of God. Some souls reach this level in thousand years.
- You mean some other souls suffer pain and loneliness, I experienced till I come here, for more than a thousand year.
- Even more according to the sins they committed. For instance Hitler, Stalin, Churchill, Truman are in this group.
- I understood first two. But why Churchill and Truman.
- If they had not decided to use nuclear weapons in Japan, people in Hiroshima and Nagasaki, who were not a threat to USA and UK, would not die hopelessly.
- Suleiman as I heard from religious people, sinners were supposed to burn in the hell. Why do they not burn?

- Have you come to that conclusion by listening to the other people or have you read Bible or Koran yourself?
- I must confess that I have come to that conclusion from the words of Muslim hocas and Christian ministers but not read any holy book. Would there be a difference if I had?
- Jesus said that he explained somethings in allegories to make his followers understand him. Koran tells exactly the same. Because the people lived at the time of holy books descended, were ignorant. They could neither understand a spherical form for world nor think of a greater pain than burning. I ask you; the loneliness, fear and curiosity you suffered till you met me. Could they not be depicted with a hell in fire? Imagine how will you feel when you will come together with your family in the afterlife realm? Could this happiness not be explained allegorically as heaven? Falling apart from beloved ones is the real hell and embracing them, is all the offerings the holy books speak about. Still Husein, if you or any other believer, had read the holy books carefully, you would not believe in burning in the hell. Christian belief says God created us in his own image. Muslims believe that all creatures will turn to God. If we are created in Lord's image or turn God finally, how can we burn in the hell?

- Suleiman if I had not met you, I would not understand any of the religious teachings. They said there are seven layers till God. Is that correct?
- It is Husein. Death means transforming human mass to universal energy. Spirituality means transforming universal energy to absolute wisdom or divine word. As physical mass is a barrier before the souls transforming into universal energy, humanly sins are barriers before transforming into divine wisdom. So we can say, universal energy is nothing but concentrated divine wisdom, as mass is originated from universal energy. That is why we should ascend through the layers for purifying our souls.
- Thank you Suleiman you enlightened me that purification is possible through the blazes of separation. But what about those Jews who were burned by Nazis. Why Lord did not protect them? If he had not, who would save them?
- Before answering your question Husein, let me show you the past lives of those Jews who were burned by Nazis.

Husein saw the images on a cloud before him. It was the prosecutor in an inquisition court.

- Honorable chairman of the court. Those 322 accused ones are Jews. They make incantation by sacrificing the goats.

They feast on some days to curse Jesus. Because they are the descendants of same people who crucified Jesus, 14 century ago. They must be executed by being burned. Court made the verdict without listening to the accused persons. They made a pile of dried woods. Young and old, women and men were screaming when they burn. The judges were laughing and congratulating each other.

- You see Husein inquisition judges committed such a big crime that their salvation would only be acceptable by the Lord, if they had been reincarnated in a Jewish body and burned by Nazis. Their souls could only be purified by this.
- Can you also tell me Suleiman if number 7 has a special meaning for the creator so that he created that many layers from earth to the divinity?
- Yes, it is a holy password in creation. That's why there are 7 main notes in an octave and 7 main colors on a rainbow. From this you should understand that music is the divine language of the Lord with which he communicates with all leaving creatures from humans to animals and plants. The colors are divine appearance of God to differentiate the creation.

30

THE FOURTH LAYER OF AFTERWORLD LIFE

After some decades passed in earthly time, Suleiman said.

- Your time is over at this layer Husein. Now you are eligible to ascend the fourth layer. We shall go to Sirius star in Orion galaxy.
- Why we go to Sirius Suleiman?
- Because the foundation of many civilizations on earth, like Atlantis, Egypt, Mesopotamia and Maya, laid down by the inhabitants of this planet. The third layer is for mentors. There, you could only see your own mentor. That is why you met me. Here, the fourth layer is for the angels or assistants of God. Many of known and unknown souls you will meet here in humanly images. You will even get in touch with them.
- For example whom can I meet?
- You can meet Ezrail, Gabriel, Seraph or even Satan. All mythological deities are also here. This stage therefore is called layer of assistants.

Suleiman and Husein walked through the trees, came near a lake. They met a tall man with long white beard. Suleiman explained Husein.

- This man was the king of the deities in pagan times.
- Suleiman, is right voyager. I was sent to earth before monotheistic religions, for humans to understand that there was a superior existence above them. Egyptians called me Ra. I was Ahuramazda in Mesopotamia, Brahma in India. Zeus in ancient Greece and Jupiter in Rome.
- Why you did not tell them that there was only one God?
- That was the wish of the creator of us. Human kind in primitive societies would not believe in something they did not see. They would not grasp the magnitude of universe nor an omnipotence force bigger and encompassing all.

Husein continued to walk along the coast line. They met a tall and healthy looking woman. She was not so beautiful but had an appearance to attract the attentions. Suleiman introduced her.

- Do you want to meet goddess of fertility Husein?
- Hello visitor. I have been long centuries in earth to grant fertility. Indians knew me as Sarasvati. In Babylon, I was Ishtar and Anahita in Persia. Romans called me Seres and Greeks Demeter. But among all these places I loved Anatolia

most. There, the people were more respectful their mother goddess than mail gods. That's why Anatolians did not call their country, fatherland but motherland. I was called Kybele in Anatolia. I was Nana when I gave birth to Phrygian king Attis. As happened in Attis my other sons also were born when I was virgin. I was Maya for Buddha and Mary for Christ. As their births, destines of my sons were the same, humans knew them as divine guides.

Husein met a lot of mythology characters during his stay.

His biggest surprise meeting came later. He met a tall, handsome and radiant young man.

- Greetings Husein. I am one of the permanent inhabitants of this place. I am Satan.
- You have been depicted by artists, as an ugly creature with horn on the forehead. I can ask you now. Why did you allure humans to commit sins? Why did you make them revolt against God?
- God is the essence of all creatures Husein. No one, can act against his orders nor can anybody exist. You will learn the meaning of sins and duties of Satan, in higher layers.
- In earthly life everybody thought of you as the enemy.
- You are right. But that is a misperception. Don't you know what Jesus said? "you will love your

enemy as well. Because God makes the sun shine on evil and good. He sends the rain drop over the unjust and the just"

- Yes I had heard it.
- O.K. then. Can I not be one of the enemies Jesus meant?

At last it was time to elevate to the fifth layer for Hüseyin.

31

THE FIFTH LAYER OF AFTERWORLD LIFE

Husein was excited. Suleiman had told him he could have the chance to meet his family. This time destination was somewhere in the Milky Way galaxy. The planet Husein found himself, after an astral voyage, was almost the same as earth. They were on a plateau surrounded by forests. They walked toward a lake. There were some people Husein could not recognize them first. When they got closer, the first time in afterlife, Husein has been happy. The women on the bank were Marlen and Peri. While he was trying to recognize the young man, Marlen shouted.

- Hasan look your father is here.

Husein was stunned. Could this, tall handsome man, be his son Hasan junior who died when he was a child? But he was so much resembling to his father Ali aga that he could not be anybody else. He experienced something exactly new. In afterlife realm, the uniting souls were increasing the field of energy and potential of souls. Husein now was covering a brighter area in the universe. Husein wondered where his parents could be. Right at that moment he recognized his mother Zeynep, a bit far away from the family group. But father Ali aga was still not there. He saw on eternity screen his father, in Saturn together with his mentor. He asked Suleiman the reason why Ali aga was in the lower layer.

The mentor opened another screen. Ali aga was wishing Happiness to Helga and Hans Peter, his best friend. He saw then, his father making love with Helga. Ali aga was betraying his best friend. He saw his father in Gallipoli informing his first wife Fatma hatun that he would marry his mother Zeynep. Fatma hatun was crying in her bed. She was complaining about her husband's behavior to God. Husein was aware now the reasons of his father's delay to elevate between the layers. He had betrayed his best friend and broken the heart of Fatma hatun. But where could be his step mother. A new screen was opened after a blinding light. Fatma hatun was giving up, her lifelong dream of pilgrimage, by spending her savings for the health care of a young boy who was praying God to grant all Fatma's wishes. But there was another man behind Fatma. Husein recognized his brother Hasan, who had lost his life in Gallipoli. He was carrying John to the trench and handing over the Australian flag to a lieutenant. Then appeared thousands of soldiers behind his brother. Husein knew this time who were they, without consulting his mentor. They were those soldiers who fought in Gallipoli without discrimination on which part they were. The enemies who killed each other on the battlefield, were at the same layer in after life realm.

- Suleiman. How could it be that my step mother Fatma, is on the same layer with my war martyr brother?
- If one sacrifices a lifelong dream for the goodness of a hopeless heart, it may be possible Husein. The most granted prayings are made by hopeless hearts.

Jenny explained further.

- For instance I met John much later than Hasan was here. I saw once my two Gallipoli veteran husbands were chatting. But Hasan was eligible to a higher layer.

Suleiman explained here.

- Husein, those who are eligible higher layers can volunteer to stay in lower ones, with the beloved ones if they wish.

They walked further. Husein met the last man he would expect to meet. He was Ismet Inonu, the second president of Turkish Republic.

- Are you here his Excellency for your achievements in the Turkish war of independence?
- Not at all. Mustafa Kemal got credit for the achievements. The reason why I am here is for my decision to send food by Kurtulus cargo ship, to hopeless and needy neighbors, by cutting from my citizens' allocations.

32

THE SIXTH LAYER OF AFTERWORLD LIFE

Husein, originally thought to stay with his family in the fifth layer. But he changed his mind recalling the words of Suleiman that one could opt lower layers to stay, returning from higher ones. If there was such a possibility why not to know the higher levels, when he is permitted?

When he arrived at the sixth layer, he was in another galaxy much farther than the Milky Way. He was stunned how a magnificent space his soul was covering. What kind of unimaginable power could create this magnitude? He felt hundreds of black points in space. He asked Suleiman.

- These are the secrets of creation Husein. These are the places where spiritual energy, forces the universal energy to condense. They are so powerful that absorb all universal energy and accumulate. As long as energy is condensed and squeezed in a hole the high pressure makes way to formation of subatomic particles? Than it burst out. In other word, a new galaxy may be born. Now I ask you to do something. Make a wish, something you dreamed of life.

Husein wished a big house near sea side in one of the friendly planets. He found himself exactly in a similar place.

Suleiman continued to explain.

- Any soul reaches sixth layer becomes spiritual master. That means you will share the divine power and order the universal energy to form into the required mass. It means whatever you think of, will be materialized in the universe as the energy transforms into mass.
- Suleiman I have never thought that God shares his power.
- God, is the wisdom behind the first creations. That means he installs the natural laws in which future creations are repeated. How do you think the musicians compose their pieces and painters or sculptors finish their art work? How do we transform steam or nuclear energy into movement?

They were already here in the universal wisdom. How can we clone a sheep or a pig? Does, being able to clone the living creatures, not mean to share the divine power?

Do you remember they told different heavens in the holy books? That meant you can select any planet or even make a new one for your afterworld life with the exact replicas of the places which you loved in your earthly life. You can stay there eternally with your beloved ones and relive your earthly memories or even materialize some of your unrealized dreams.

- Do you mean I or any other soul can have their own planet to actualize their earthly dreams in the afterworld life. Is it not a huge burden for the Lord?
- It is surely huge but not a burden for the Lord whose power is limitless Husein. Remember when you left the earth, world population was 7 billion. Recollect now your earthly knowledge. Each human had a different eye retina. Each person could be discriminated from his unique voice vibration. Detectives could distinguish the criminals from their identical finger prints. Dogs recognized their masters from their smell. Astrologists found connections between the locations of the planets and the days of our birth. Some others told our destiny just analyzing the lines in our palms. So much every detail is destined by the Lord that he creates each of his creatures differently, in all aspects.
- But Suleiman if everything is destined by God there should not be evil and good nor sinners or innocents. If each soul will arrive sooner or

later at highest layer, there should not be even heaven and hell. Should there be?

- It is time now for you to know the divine reality Husein. The purpose of creation is to make the Lord known by humans. Imagine, at the very beginning there was an almighty existence who had omnipotence but not known and alone in vacancy. He wanted to be known in billion different ways. That could only be possible by creating everything in contrasts and sharing his wisdom. For this reason, there should be good and evil at the same time. Some people were destined to be allured by Satan and were punished in earth or afterworld life. This way they know god with punishment after committing a sin. Some others were ready to be guided by angels. They are destined to make good deeds and rewarded by the benevolences of the Lord in the life or afterworld.

- Do you mean we shall recollect all our earthly deeds, be it good or evil in afterlife world?

- Remember Husein how many good memories you had on earth you want to live on and bad experiences you want to forget. This is the place where you will continue to live in good memories forever.

- How could then be punishment in afterworld life?

- Sometimes forgiving is shortened by reincarnation of the souls to be punished second time in the world against their first time wrongdoings. I showed you previously inquisition judges who ordered to burn

217

the Jews in their first lives. They could purified their souls by being born second time and tortured in Nazi's Germany. You learned Husein now the reasons of being driven to act evil and good. You learned why there is Satan and angels. Do you want to continue to the seventh layer?

- Suleiman if one could opt lower layers to stay, returning from higher ones. If there is such a possibility why should I not know the higher levels, as much as I am permitted.

- O.K. Husein. You should know that by ascending the seventh layer you will find greater souls than me to answer your questions. Ascending to the ultimate layer means to encompass the whole universe at the limits of the Lord. At the seventh layer you will have two choices. You will either stay there by losing all your identities or prefer to stay at a lower layer and help development of universal changes within your destiny.

33

THE SEVENTH LAYER OF AFTERWORLD LIFE

When arrived seventh layer Husein was both amazed and restless. His soul was covering now the whole universe. Coming to the sixth layer he had passed two galaxies. But now there were a lot of galaxies in front of him. He then realized that he had grasped part of the universe clearer and stronger till sixth layer. Here the vision was endless but clarity was weak. Suleiman explained.

- Be it Christian or Muslim, believers thought that ascending to God was something to climb a ladder and on top of the hill there was heaven and God. This explanation was good for humans in primitive societies. But when man learned electromagnetic waves, it was ridiculous to make believe that God is squeezed in a certain spot of the universe though he created all. You can perceive the whole universe now. Do you know why? Because God created everything from his own spiritual existence. You were, till sixth layer, a drop in the ocean. But by returning your original source of spirituality, you have become an ocean in a drop now. Neither Satan nor angels, humans, mountains, planets and galaxies were originated from a different source, but God. You were surprised in sixth layer by your might, to bring anything you may think of, in front of you. But here in the seventh layer get ready for further surprises. For instance whom you wanted to meet most in life? Think of him.

Husein most wanted person to meet was Mevlana Celaleddin Rumi, the well esteemed mystique poet. The moment he thought of him he saw Mevlana and asked him his vital question striking his soul.

- I have ascended to this level great Mevlana but I cannot decide whether I should stay here or opt to be with my family in the fifth layer?

He was expecting the answer from him. Instead, he perceived what Mevlana would answer, inside his soul.

- If you were a selfish man in life who lived for yourself stay with your family. The ultimate 7th layer is, for those who in life, had been sad with the sorrow of humans and been happy with their joys. Those who saw God in all earthly existence, be it a garden in the spring, the sun set time in the twilight or moon light on the sea. Those who listened the songs as the voice of the Lord, smelled the flowers and tasted the fruits as heavenly pleasures are the permanent abiders of this layer. Because in this layer there is no personal wish but adaptation to the divine destiny and be part of it.

Husein could not grasp those words quickly. Instead he asked an easy question.

- What will be the future of Turkey great Mevlana?
- You don't need to worry about the future of Turks since you are the people from Anatolia which is the birth place of human kind and civilizations. Old Testament said Adam and Eve were settled between Tigris and Euphrates rivers when they were expelled from heaven. Bible informed Noah arch came to rest on Ararat Mountain after the big flood. Koran told that Abraham put on fire and did not burn in Anatolia. Stories of archaeology continued where the religion stopped. A 12.000 year old settlement site was explored where Abraham once lived. That's why God protects and favors Anatolians. Interesting part of the conversation was, Husein was not only answering his question on Mevlana behalf

but he was acquiring his mind as well. Suleiman explained the miracle.

- Don't get so much amazed Husein. In this layer there is no you and me. Everything and everybody is we. Because all of us at this layer have been part of the divine spirituality.
- Why then, there has been so many wars, in which so many young men lost lives? Why the humans from different races and religions could not come along, to live a peaceful life? An incredible thing happened after his thought. Jesus and Mohammed appeared at once. Husein asked Jesus.
- Oh Jesus. Why humans kill each other? Why super powers use nuclear and biological weapons on weak ones? Why Lord doesn't protect hopelessly innocent people?

Mohammed answered instead of Jesus.

- Unfortunately Husein neither Jesus nor Mohammed words were clearly understood by their followers. We said "If you love your enemy you can be the children of the father." What Christians and Muslims mostly did was to kill humans instead of caring and loving them. Muslims made even worst. They fabricated false words from Mohammed provoking war against non-Muslims.

Jesus continued exactly where Mohammed finished.

- The humanly instinct of being superior, caused all conflicts and tragedies. But ultimately this instinct was granted by God as one of the purposes of creation. God created universe and humans in contrasts, to make things known. We could not know the heat if we had not experienced cold. We would not try to be passionate if we had not suffered from hate. How we could differentiate good from evil, if some people had not thanked God for his benevolences while the others hopelessly pray for salvation. That is why Satan is needed as angels. We are driven to commit sins by satanic deceive and punished in corporeal or spiritual life. That causes us to know the divine existence. We are rewarded after our good deeds in earth or afterworld life that makes us believe in divine justice.

Husein asked the last question in his mind.

- In holy books there is a concept of doomsday when all corpses spring out from their graves to be questioned for judgement. Are these verses wrong?
- No verse in holy books is wrong even if they are descended for most primitive societies but most are allegorical explanations to make the ignorant

people understand. Doomsday is awakening to reality. But no one, should expect that we shall come back to world for salvation or to establish order in the world. Irresponsible acts would only be corrected by the responsible deeds of concerned ones after a mark of warning. Some calls it punishment. You knew Husein by your own experience that there has never been death in afterworld life. It is actually transformation of corporeal mass into energy. But how could people animate this, in their minds before the relativity theory of Einstein? Doomsday is the elevation to seventh layer afterworld life. It is the ultimate awakening after experiencing all the sufferings through the layers which could be attributed to the blazes of hell. That is why we should not insult the sinners as they may be more pain sufferers than good souls.

- In my life I heard several times that religion and science are contradicting concepts.
- This is the biggest misconception Husein. Scientific facts are the rules of God. Holy books are the allegories could be interpreted separately according to the level of knowledge of the people. That means further human kind progress in science, better the verses will be interpreted.
- Do you mean religion should come to the same conclusion with Darwin in evolution theory?

- Those object Darwin, are in the same situation with those claimed a flat world. After drawing the gene maps of animals, it has been proven that monkeys carry 99,9 % of the same genes as humans. In holy books we can find many times the story of Adam and Eve about eating the forbidden fruit in heaven. But few stories are told about their life in the world. You can find the connection, if you carefully study the holy books. They should be understood as God made all living creatures by evolution and when came to the apes he blew his breath to implant humanly wisdom into the apes who could be called Adam as well. If you wish to translate religious term into scientific one, you may say blowing is equal to mutation. But you could not explain mutation to the people in primitive societies. Ministers interpreted it as God came down to earth to shape Adam from mud. The real difference between scientists and religion is that they say mutation is accidental selection. They mostly do not accept divine design, which is pure stupidity on their behalf. If creation in the universe has been accidental, could macro cosmos be exactly in the same form as micro cosmos. Could the electrons and protons around the nucleus of an atom navigate the same way satellites do around the suns?

Suleiman interfered here

- Husein now it is the time to make a decision. Will you stay at seventh layer or do you prefer to descend the lower layrs to be with your beloved ones forever?
- I will opt to be near my beloved ones.

E N D